Practical Approaches to Literary Criticism

general editor
Richard Adams

Novels

Robert Wilson

Longman

Longman Group UK Limited,
*Longman House, Burnt Mill, Harlow,
Essex CM20 2JE, England
and Associated Companies throughout the world.*

First published 1987

*Set in 10/12pt Linotron 202 Baskerville
Produced by Longman Group (FE) Ltd
Printed in Hong Kong*

ISBN 0 582 35530 3

20 04009495

Acknowledgements

We are grateful to the following for permission to reproduce copyright
material:

Edward Arnold Ltd for extracts from *A Passage to India* by
E. M. Forster; Jonathan Cape Ltd on behalf of the James Joyce Estate
& The Society of Authors as Literary Representatives of the James
Joyce Estate for extracts from *The Dubliners* by James Joyce; Chatto &
Windus Ltd & Mrs. Laura Huxley for extracts from *Brave New World*
by Aldous Huxley; Faber & Faber Ltd for extracts from *Lord of the
Flies* by William Golding & *The Bell Jar* by Sylvia Plath; Wm
Heinemann Ltd for extracts from *To Kill a Mocking Bird* by Harper
Lee; The Hogarth Press for the Author's Estate for extracts from *To
the Lighthouse* by Virginia Woolf; authors' agents on behalf of the
Estate of the late Sonia Brownell Orwell & Secker & Warburg Ltd for
extracts from *Nineteen Eighty Four* by George Orwell.

Contents

5 *Narrative* 96

Introduction

This book will encourage post-GCSE students to read and discuss extracts from novels in a sensitive and perceptive way. It introduces them to the work of many of the major novelists and to a couple of less well-known writers and so offers a taste of the great tradition of the English novel.

It is hoped that students will gain an appreciation of some of the narrative and descriptive techniques that are most frequently employed by novelists and that this understanding will enable them to approach the analysis of prose extracts with clarity and confidence.

Although the treatment of entire novels is beyond the scope of this book, it will stimulate students to read further in the writings of the classical novelists and to be aware of how such matters as narrative stance, characterisation and situation are developed in the wider context of the whole novel.

Finally, since a thematic organisation of the choice of extracts has been applied in the first four chapters, it is hoped that students will come to recognise the relevance of the study of novels to the real concerns of our individual and corporate lives, to the deeper understanding of our relationships with ourselves, with each other and with the societies in which we live.

1 Alone

Prose fiction is invariably about people and, at its best, it explores personality, not merely presenting us with simple caricatured patterns of human behaviour, people reduced to the crude formulae of 'the villain' or 'the reliable good guy' or 'the beautiful girl' or 'the stupid old woman'. Novels may demand our acute attention to very complex shifts of feeling and awareness within the characters under scrutiny. In this chapter we shall consider three episodes from twentieth-century novels concerning the intense experiences of a teenage girl, a small boy and an old lady.

Despair

In *The Bell Jar* by Sylvia Plath, a young American girl suffers disillusionment with her life and circumstances, finds that she is unable to communicate with other people and unwilling to try. She cannot create anything that satisfies her and self-destruction presents itself as the obvious expression of her state of being. But, before she attempts suicide, she prepares herself by visiting her father's grave. **I suggest that you examine the following extract and, before going on to read my further comments on it, you either discuss it or write about it with the following points in mind:**

1   what we learn of the heroine's present state of mind and feelings
2   what we learn of her family background and of her attitude to her parents
3   the structure of the passage with its odd connections between different sections and its digressions
4   the tone created through the use of the first person narra-

1

tive form. Would the effect have been very different if these events had been described by a third-person narrator?

I had a great yearning, lately, to pay my father back for all the years of neglect, and start tending his grave. I had always been my father's favourite, and it seemed fitting I should take on a mourning my mother had never bothered with.

I thought that if my father hadn't died, he would have taught me all about insects, which was his speciality at the university. He would also have taught me German and Greek and Latin, which he knew, and perhaps I would be a Lutheran. My father had been a Lutheran in Wisconsin, but they were out of style in New England, so he had become a lapsed Lutheran and then, my mother said, a bitter atheist.

The graveyard disappointed me. It lay at the outskirts of the town, on low ground, like a rubbish dump, and as I walked up and down the gravel paths, I could smell the stagnant salt marshes in the distance.

The old part of the graveyard was all right, with its worn, flat stones and lichen-bitten monuments, but I soon saw my father must be buried in the modern part with dates in the 1940's.

The stones in the modern part were crude and cheap, and here and there a grave was rimmed with marble, like an oblong bathtub full of dirt, and rusty metal containers stuck up about where the person's navel would be, full of plastic flowers.

A fine drizzle started drifting down from the grey sky, and I grew very depressed.

I couldn't find my father anywhere.

Low, shaggy clouds scudded over that part of the horizon where the sea lay, behind the marshes and the beach shanty settlements, and raindrops darkened the black mackintosh I had bought that morning. A clammy dampness sank through to my skin.

I had asked the salegirl, 'Is it water-repellent?'

And she had said, 'No raincoat is ever water-*repellent*: It's showerproofed.'

And when I asked her what showerproofed was, she told me I had better buy an umbrella.

40 But I hadn't enough money for an umbrella. What with bus fare in and out of Boston and peanuts and newspapers and abnormal psychology books and trips to my old home town by the sea, my New York fund was almost exhausted.

I had decided that when there was no more money in my bank account I would do it, and that morning I'd spent the last of it on the black raincoat.

Then I saw my father's gravestone.

It was crowded right up by another gravestone, head 50 to head, the way people are crowded in a charity ward when there isn't enough space. The stone was of a mottled pink marble, like tinned salmon, and all there was on it was my father's name and, under it, two dates, separated by a little dash.

At the foot of the stone I arranged the rainy armful of azaleas I had picked from a bush at the gateway of the graveyard. Then my legs folded under me, and I sat down in the sopping grass. I couldn't understand why I was crying so hard.

60 Then I remembered that I had never cried for my father's death.

My mother hadn't cried either. She had just smiled and said what a merciful thing it was for him he had died, because if he had lived he would have been crippled and an invalid for life, and he couldn't have stood that, he would rather have died than had that happen.

I laid my face to the smooth face of the marble and howled my loss into the cold salt rain.

I knew just how to go about it.

70 The minute the car tyres crunched off down the drive and the sound of the motor faded, I jumped out of bed and hurried into my white blouse and green figured skirt and black raincoat. The raincoat felt damp still, from the day before, but that would soon cease to matter.

I went downstairs and picked up a pale blue envelope from the dining-room table and scrawled on the back, in large, painstaking letters: *I am going for a long walk.*

I propped the message where my mother would see it the minute she came in.

80 Then I laughed.

I had forgotten the most important thing.

I ran upstairs and dragged a chair into my mother's closet. Then I climbed and reached for the small green strongbox on the top shelf. I could have torn the metal cover off with my bare hands, the lock was so feeble, but I wanted to do things in a calm, orderly way.

I pulled out my mother's upper right-hand bureau drawer and slipped the blue jewellery box from its hiding-place under the scented Irish linen handkerchiefs.

90 I unpinned the little key from the dark velvet. Then I unlocked the strongbox and took out the bottle of new pills. There were more than I had hoped.

There were at least fifty.

If I had waited until my mother doled them out to me, night by night, it would have taken me fifty nights to save up enough. And in fifty nights, college would have opened, and my brother would have come back from Germany, and it would be too late.

I pinned the key back in the jewellery box among the

100 clutter of inexpensive chains and rings, put the jewellery box back in the drawer under the handkerchiefs, returned the strongbox to the closet shelf and set the chair on the rug in the exact spot I had dragged it from.

Then I went downstairs and into the kitchen. I turned on the tap and poured myself a tall glass of water. Then I took the glass of water and the bottle of pills and went down into the cellar.

A dim, undersea light filtered through the slits of the cellar windows. Behind the oil burner, a dark gap showed in the wall at about shoulder height and ran back under the breezeway, out of sight. The breezeway had been added to the house after the cellar was dug, and built out over this secret, earth-bottomed crevice.

A few old, rotting fireplace logs blocked the hole mouth. I shoved them back a bit. Then I set the glass of water and the bottle of pills side by side on the flat surface of one of the logs and started to heave myself up.

It took me a good while to heft my body into the gap, but at last, after many tries, I managed it, and crouched at the mouth of the darkness, like a troll.

The earth seemed friendly under my bare feet, but cold. I wondered how long it had been since this particular square of soil had seen the sun.

Then, one after the other, I lugged the heavy, dust-covered logs across the hole mouth. The dark felt thick as velvet. I reached for the glass and bottle, and carefully, on my knees, with bent head, crawled to the farthest wall.

Cobwebs touched my face with the softness of moths. Wrapping my black coat round me like my own sweet shadow, I unscrewed the bottle of pills and started taking them swiftly, between gulps of water, one by one by one.

At first nothing happened, but as I approached the bottom of the bottle, red and blue lights began to flash before my eyes. The bottle slid from my fingers and I lay down.

The silence drew off, baring the pebbles and shells and

5

140   all the tatty wreckage of my life. Then, at the rim of
vision, it gathered itself, and in one sweeping tide, rushed
me to sleep.

Sylvia Plath, *The Bell Jar* (1963)

I shall confine my comments to the first half of the extract –
the visit to the graveyard – so leaving you the opportunity to
explore and write a detailed appreciation of the rest of the
passage.

This is a piece of 'confessional' writing. It presents us with
a mass of personal experience unadorned by comment or
analysis. As we read this novel we are inevitably in the position
of the psycho-analyst or the counsellor who listens to
someone's life story and tries to make sense of what is going
on. We must attend to the manner in which information is
given to us as well as to its content and it is the manner of
the narration in this book which perhaps strikes us first. The
heroine describes the most traumatic and dramatic events in
an almost completely bland and unemotional way. She gives
us information about her father – that he died young, that he
was a university teacher, that he had lost his faith – and about
her mother's callous failure to mourn his death but, although
she speculates about what her father might have meant to her
('He would also have taught me German and Greek and Latin,
which he knew, and perhaps I would be a Lutheran . . .' lines
8–10), for most of the passage she tells us nothing of her
feelings.

Put yourself for a moment in her position. You might be
feeling angry that you had been deprived of a loving father,
regretful that there was not the guidance and meaning in your
life that he might have represented and you might well feel
hatred and bitterness towards a mother who was unmoved by
her husband's death, regarding it as a matter of convenience,
and who paid no attention to his grave or to any mourning
of his loss. Yet this girl shows few feelings on the surface and

that, in itself, may be a cause of her attempted suicide: since she can feel nothing, life seems empty and meaningless.

One result of her detachment from feelings is the odd way she uses language. She reproduces, verbatim and without comment, the clichés and standard responses of other people and this creates a type of sad humour. Her father's whole spiritual history is reduced to the inadequate clichés provided by her mother – 'a lapsed Lutheran', 'a bitter atheist' – and that's that! Similarly, the amusing digression on the purchase of her mackintosh coolly describes, and by implication condemns, the irritation of a shopgirl who can only deal in standard phrases like 'water-repellent' and 'showerproofed' and who rejects the narrator's desire to approach some sort of truth about the raincoat. She appears to hate the superficial, the artificial, whether it be evident in the words of other people or in objects. So, there are a number of wryly detached observations about the graveyard: how a grave was 'rimmed with marble, like an oblong bathtub full of dirt, and rusty metal containers stuck up about where the person's navel would be, full of plastic flowers'. What is the tone of this comment? Scorn, dislike, an underlying desire to get at the truth of things, to remind herself of the body that lies beneath the soil and to express dislike of the tastelessness and artificiality of the place? Notice how the same down-to-earth, debunking tone emerges when she finds her father's grave. With what does she compare the crowding together of the graves and what feelings does that comparison evoke? With what does she compare the colour of the marble stone?

The first episode of this extract culminates at a point where feelings finally break through. We are told, 'Then my legs folded under me and I sat down in the sopping grass. I couldn't understand why I was crying so hard (lines 57–59).' She seems surprised to discover that she has any feelings and it is as if she observes her own emotional discharge from a distance, providing herself with a reason, an explanation for her sorrow. The final sentence of the section is moving and it gathers together a number of implied thoughts: 'I laid my face to the smooth face of the marble and howled my loss into the cold salt rain.' For what is she crying? Her 'loss' is the loss of her father and of so much more. She has endured emotional deprivations that have left her completely isolated. Laying her face against the smooth face of the marble emphasises – in the repetition of 'face' – how hard she has been required to be and yet how different is a person from a block of stone. She needs comfort but the only 'face' available to her is this unfeeling marble. She 'howls', not 'cries', and the word suggests some primitive animal instinct which has taken over. Finally, all this occurs in the cold and wet. The setting is important; it reinforces the sense that there is no warmth nor comfort for her in anything.

Now, confine your attention to the second half of the extract – the description of the narrator's attempted suicide – and write an appreciation of it in which you describe:

1 the way she set about killing herself
2 what she thinks or feels or notices at different moments and, in particular, what she feels about the hole in the earth in which she lies
3 the effects created by the various comparisons, the similes and metaphors, that she uses
4 the way the event is written; that is, notice the sort of sentences and paragraphs that Sylvia Plath employs and say why they are appropriate for her purpose.

Confrontation

William Golding's *Lord of the Flies* concerns a party of school-boys which is marooned on a tropical island as a result of an aeroplane crash. One group of the boys becomes absorbed in hunting, with increasing savagery, the wild boar they find on the island whilst a couple of more responsible boys do all they can to stem this frightening tide of violence and look for ways of organising their corporate life. But all of them fear the darkness and the unknown; they feel the presence of something dangerous on the island and this they call 'the beast'. So, when the hunters at last succeed in killing a pig, they decapitate it and fix its head on a stick as an offering to this supposed beast. One boy, Simon, more reflective than the rest, resists this simple and superstitious reduction of the evil in life to a 'beast' which he knows does not exist. In these extracts we see him struggling to hold on to his sense of there being far deeper truths about human nature.

Simon stayed where he was, a small brown image, concealed by the leaves. Even if he shut his eyes the sow's head still remained like an after-image. The half-shut eyes were dim with the infinite cynicism of adult life. They assured Simon that everything was a bad business.
'I know that.'

Simon discovered that he had spoken aloud. He opened his eyes quickly and there was the head grinning amusedly in the strange daylight, ignoring the flies, the
10 spilled guts, even ignoring the indignity of being spiked on a stick.

He looked away, licking his dry lips.

A gift for the beast. Might not the beast come for it? The head, he thought, appeared to agree with him. Run away, said the head silently, go back to the others. It was a joke really – why should you bother? You were just wrong, that's all. A little headache, something you ate, perhaps. Go back, child, said the head silently.

Simon looked up, feeling the weight of his wet hair,
20 and gazed at the sky. Up there, for once, were clouds, great bulging towers that sprouted away over the island,

grey and cream and copper-coloured. The clouds were
sitting on the land; they squeezed, produced moment by
moment, this close, tormenting heat. Even the butterflies
deserted the open space where the obscene thing grinned
and dripped. Simon lowered his head, carefully keeping
his eyes shut, then sheltered them with his hand. There
were no shadows under the trees but everywhere a pearly
stillness, so that what was real seemed illusive and
30   without definition. The pile of guts was a black blob of
flies that buzzed like a saw. After a while these flies found
Simon. Gorged, they alighted by his runnels of sweat and
drank. They tickled under his nostrils and played leap-
frog on his thighs. They were black and iridescent green
and without number; and in front of Simon, the Lord
of the Flies hung on his stick and grinned. At last Simon
gave up and looked back; saw the white teeth and dim
eyes, the blood – and his gaze was held by that ancient,
inescapable recognition. In Simon's right temple, a pulse
40   began to beat on the brain.

William Golding, Lord of the Flies (1954)

Simon meditates in an intensely imaginative and painful way
on the nature of evil. He takes the external reality of the sow's
head stuck on a stick into his own inner being, for we are told
that 'Even if he shut his eyes the sow's head remained like
an after-image' (lines 2–3). As this image becomes part of
him, it enables him to commune with himself. He verbalises
his sense of the evil in life, though he expresses it initially
through the weak statement that 'everything was a bad business' (line 5). Consider how hollow, how ordinary the saying
sounds: that clichéd response is one way whereby men seek to
weaken the fact, the problem of evil. It is the attitude of those
who have lost all idealism, all hope for improving things and
who simply allow life to take its course. This is the 'infinite
cynicism of adult life' (line 4) – since things are such a bad

business there's no point in thinking you can alter anything; just go with the crowd and stop bothering – and these are precisely the sentiments that Simon imagines the pig's head to be expressing (lines 12–16). Will Simon accept this message? Will he cease to struggle for truth? Will he capitulate and 'go back to the others', dismissing his insight as no more than a headache, a mere physical upset? **Look again at the passage with this issue in mind and consider the following questions**:

1 How does Golding create an atmosphere of evil which intensifies our sense of Simon's inner conflict? Which details of the physical circumstances add to the intensity? All the descriptive details of the final paragraph of the extract above need analysis.

2 How do we know that Simon is fighting to hold on to his grasp of reality? How exactly do you interpret the penultimate sentence of the extract (lines 36–39)?

Immediately following the passage I have quoted from *Lord of the Flies*, there are a few pages describing the activities of some of the other boys on the island. Then Golding returns us to Simon and his confrontation with the pig's skull, the 'Lord of the Flies'. Simon is, in fact, epileptic and we now realise (line 32) that he is in the early stages of a fit.

Write an interpretation of the following passage bringing out the way in which Simon's moral struggle is dramatised by the situation that Golding develops.

'You are a silly little boy,' said the Lord of the Flies, 'just an ignorant, silly little boy.'

Simon moved his swollen tongue but said nothing.

11

'Don't you agree?' said the Lord of the Flies. 'Aren't you just a silly little boy?'

Simon answered him in the same silent voice.

'Well then,' said the Lord of the Flies, 'you'd better run off and play with the others. They think you're batty. You don't want Ralph to think you're batty, do you? You like Ralph a lot, don't you? And Piggy, and Jack?'

Simon's head was tilted slightly up. His eyes could not break away and the Lord of the Flies hung in space before him.

'What are you doing out here all alone? Aren't you afraid of me?'

Simon shook.

'There isn't anyone to help you. Only me. And I'm the Beast.'

Simon's mouth laboured, brought forth audible words.

'Pig's head on a stick.'

'Fancy thinking the Beast was something you could hunt and kill!' said the head. For a moment or two the forest and all the other dimly appreciated places echoed with the parody of laughter. 'You knew, didn't you? I'm part of you? Close, close, close! I'm the reason why it's no go? Why things are what they are?'

The laughter shivered again.

'Come now,' said the Lord of the Flies. 'Get back to the others and we'll forget the whole thing.'

Simon's head wobbled. His eyes were half-closed as though he were imitating the obscene thing on the stick. He knew that one of his times was coming on. The Lord of the Flies was expanding like a balloon.

'This is ridiculous. You know perfectly well you'll only meet me down there – so don't try to escape!'

Simon's body was arched and stiff. The Lord of the Flies spoke in the voice of a schoolmaster.

'This has gone quite far enough. My poor, misguided child, do you think you know better than I do?'

40   There was a pause.

'I'm warning you. I'm going to get waxy. D'you see? You're not wanted. Understand? We are going to have fun on this island. Understand? We are going to have fun on this island! So don't try it on, my poor misguided boy, or else – '

Simon found he was looking into a vast mouth. There was blackness within, a blackness that spread.

' – Or else,' said the Lord of the Flies, 'we shall do you. See? Jack and Roger and Maurice and Robert and
50   Bill and Piggy and Ralph. Do you. See?'

Simon was inside the mouth. He fell down and lost consciousness.

William Golding, *Lord of the Flies* (1954)

Meaninglessness

The extracts from *The Bell Jar* and *Lord of the Flies* are turning points in those novels: neither character will be the same after these experiences. The same is true of what is a central event in *A Passage to India* by E M Forster. This is an outing to visit some caves, the main characters of the sightseeing party being Dr Aziz, a young Indian who has organised the trip, and Miss Adela Quested and Mrs Moore, two English ladies visiting India, the former quite young and the latter elderly.

The first cave was tolerably convenient. They skirted the puddle of water, and then climbed up over some unattractive stones, the sun crashing on their backs. Bending their heads, they disappeared one by one into the interior of the hills. The small black hole gaped where their varied forms and colours had momentarily functioned. They were sucked in like water down a drain.

Bland and bald rose the precipices; bland and glutinous the sky that connected the precipices; solid and white, a Brahmany kite flapped between the rocks with a clumsiness that seemed intentional. Before man, with his itch for the seemly, had been born, the planet must have looked thus. The kite flapped away . . . Before birds, perhaps . . . And then the hole belched, and humanity returned.

A Marabar cave had been horrid as far as Mrs Moore was concerned, for she had nearly fainted in it, and had some difficulty in preventing herself from saying so as soon as she got into the air again. It was natural enough: she had always suffered from faintness, and the cave had become too full, because all their retinue followed them. Crammed with villagers and servants, the circular chamber began to smell. She lost Aziz and Adela in the dark, didn't know who touched her, couldn't breathe, and some vile naked thing struck her face and settled on her mouth like a pad. She tried to regain the entrance tunnel, but an influx of villagers swept her back. She hit her head. For an instant she went mad, hitting and gasping like a fanatic. For not only did the crush and stench alarm her; there was also a terrifying echo.

Professor Godbole had never mentioned an echo; it never impressed him, perhaps. There are some exquisite echoes in India; there is the whisper round the dome at Bijapur; there are the long, solid sentences that voyage through the air at Mandu, and return unbroken to their creator. The echo in a Marabar cave is not like these, it is entirely devoid of distinction. Whatever is said, the same monotonous noise replies, and quivers up and down the walls until it is absorbed into the roof. 'Boum' is the sound as far as the human alphabet can express it, or 'bou-oum', or 'ou-boum' – utterly dull. Hope, politeness, the blowing of a nose, the squeak of a boot, all produce 'boum'. Even the striking of a match starts a little worm coiling, which is too small to complete a circle, but is eternally watchful. And if several people talk at once an overlapping howling noise begins, echoes generate echoes, and the cave is stuffed with a snake composed of small snakes, which writhe independently.

50   After Mrs Moore all the others poured out. She had given the signal for the reflux. Aziz and Adela both emerged smiling and she did not want him to think his treat was a failure, so smiled too. As each person emerged she looked for a villain, but none was there, and she realized that she had been among the mildest individuals, whose only desire was to honour her, and that the naked pad was a poor little baby, astride its mother's hip. Nothing evil had been in the cave, but she had not enjoyed herself; no, she had not enjoyed herself,
60   and she decided not to visit a second one.

E M Forster, *A Passage to India* (1924)

When you have read and pondered on this passage as a whole, I suggest you take each of its four paragraphs in turn and analyse it in detail using the relevant questions to guide your thinking.

1   In the first paragraph, consider
   (a)   the effect in their context of the words 'crashing', 'sucked', 'gaped', 'belched'.
   (b)   the tone of the first sentence and its relationship with Forster's mention of 'man, with his itch for the seemly'.
   (c)   the effect of repetitions of words and phrases.
   (d)   why Forster includes the description of the kite.
   (e)   above all, what he is implying in this paragraph about man and his place in creation.

2   In the second paragraph, identify precisely what has

happened to Mrs Moore in the cave and how she recalls the experience afterwards. What seems to be the cause of her upset? Upon which details does her revulsion against the experience fasten?

3 (a) Who is speaking in the third paragraph?
   (b) Why is there a digression on 'the echoes of India'?
   (c) Which sentence most forcefully sums up the effect of an echo in the Marabar caves?
   (d) What use does Forster make of the image of the snake? Why is it appropriate and how does he develop it?

4 How do the style and concerns of the fourth paragraph differ from those of the third? Try to define Mrs Moore's state of mind and feeling at this point. Has she satisfactorily resolved the upset she had felt in the cave? Attempt now to judge what is 'the truth' of that upset and whether Mrs Moore is now rationalising her experience, that is, merely explaining it away, or gaining insight from it.

After this extract, Aziz and Adela go on to visit another cave whilst Mrs Moore excuses herself, is pleasant and helpful to Aziz, and sinks into a deckchair in the shade to await their return . . .

If they reached the big pocket of caves, they would be away nearly an hour. She took out her writing-pad and began, 'Dear Stella, Dear Ralph,' then stopped, and looked at the queer valley and their feeble invasion of it. Even the elephant had become a nobody. Her eye rose from it to the entrance tunnel. No, she did not wish to repeat that experience. The more she thought over it, the more disagreeable and frightening it became. She minded it much more now than at the time. The crush and the smells she could forget, but the echo began in some indescribable way to undermine her hold on life. Coming at a moment when she chanced to be fatigued, it had managed to murmur: 'Pathos, piety, courage – they exist, but are identical, and so is filth. Everything exists, nothing has value.' If one had spoken vileness in that place, or quoted lofty poetry, the comment would have been the same – 'ou-boum'. If one had spoken with the tongues of angels and pleaded for all the unhappiness and misunderstanding in the world, past, present, and to come, for all the misery men must undergo whatever their opinion and position, and however much they dodge or bluff – it would amount to the same, the serpent would descend and return to the ceiling. Devils are of the North, and poems can be written about them, but no one could romanticize the Marabar, because it robbed infinity and eternity of their vastness, the only quality that accommodates them to mankind.

She tried to go on with her letter, reminding herself that she was only an elderly woman who had got up too early in the morning and journeyed too far, that the despair creeping over her was merely her despair, her personal weakness, and that even if she got a sunstroke and went mad the rest of the world would go on. But suddenly, at the edge of her mind, Religion appeared, poor little talkative Christianity, and she knew that all its divine words from 'Let there be light' to 'It is finished' only amounted to 'boum'. Then she was terrified over an area larger than usual; the universe, never comprehensible to her intellect, offered no repose to her soul, the mood of the last two months took definite form at last, and she realized that she didn't want to write to her children, didn't want to communicate with anyone, not even with God. She sat motionless with horror, and, when old Mohammed Latif came up to her, thought he would notice a difference. For a time she thought, 'I am going to be ill,' to comfort herself, then she surrendered to the vision. She lost all interest, even in Aziz, and the affectionate and sincere words that she had spoken to him seemed no longer hers but the air's.

E M Forster, *A Passage to India* (1924)

Notice how, in the course of these two paragraphs, we move in and out of Mrs Moore's mind. At some points the author is obviously commenting directly on the nature of the experience; at other times we seem to know Mrs Moore's own thoughts. Go through this extract and identify those statements which constitute Forster's commentary on Mrs Moore's experience. What is he saying? Some of his statements are not easy to understand. What do you make of the final sentence of the first paragraph?

Now turn your attention to the actions and thoughts of Mrs Moore. With which actions and with which thoughts does she seek to keep at bay the frightening realisations that have broken into her mind? Try to plot the precise sequence of her thoughts and define the nature of the vision to which she finally surrenders herself.

Write an appreciation of the extracts from *A Passage to India* creating comparisons, if you wish, between them and the extracts from *Lord of the Flies*.

Finally, review your reactions to all the extracts in this chapter. The following questions may stimulate some discussion.

1 Which of the three characters do you feel you know best? Which is most clearly individualised? How?
2 In which passage do you have the strongest sense of surroundings? Is this equally powerful or important in each of the three episodes?
3 Which author seems most concerned to universalise the experience of the individual character?
4 Compare the tone, the way of speaking, in each passage.

For example, which is the most detached, the most refined, the most serious in tone?

5   How do you think each of these three characters will feel and live after these events are past? In particular, think about how their relationships with the people around them and with society as a whole will be affected by these experiences. This will lead us naturally on to the issue of the next chapter.

2 Societies

When we say we 'know' someone, we may mean one of at least two things: it may be that we 'know' the person privately and have an understanding of her or his character and individuality, that we might be aware of the sort of inner, personal life that we explored in the last chapter but, equally, it may be that we 'know' someone as part of a society, in terms of the individual's role or occupation in public life. In the latter case, income, class, pattern of relationships, job, style of living, style of speaking, accent and political attitudes – and much else – may all be relevant to our 'placing' of that person in society. This dimension of our lives is inescapable and infinitely complex and each of us plays out a drama of interrelationship with the society in which we live, finding it sometimes inhibiting to the development of our sense of individuality and at other times encouraging to the growth of our talents and self-expression. These are the matters that we shall be looking at in this chapter, for if a novel presents us with a number of characters in relationship with each other, then it must almost inevitably convey a particular view of a society. And the society created in a novel may well be far more than a background to the events, a sort of stage setting against which the characters move; its values and attitudes are likely to be a central issue.

Toleration

We start with an extract from a pleasantly humorous novel which does nevertheless contain serious undercurrents. *To Kill a Mockingbird* by Harper Lee is set in the American deep South. The narrator recalls her childhood in the small American community of Maycomb, Alabama, where her father, Atticus Finch, is the town lawyer. She has an older brother, Jem, and, since her mother is dead, Calpurnia, the black housekeeper, is an important part of her world. Jean Louise, the narrator, is known as 'Scout' to her friends and family. The following extract presents some of her experience on her first day at school where her teacher, Miss Caroline, who is new to the town, is also starting her first term of teaching at the school. Just before the extract begins, Scout has irritated Miss Caroline by revealing that, having been taught by her father and Calpurnia, she can already read and write.

'Everybody who goes home to lunch hold up your hands,' said Miss Caroline, breaking into my new grudge against Calpurnia.

The town children did so, and she looked us over.

'Everybody who brings his lunch put it on top of his desk.'

Molasses buckets appeared from nowhere, and the ceiling danced with metallic light. Miss Caroline walked up and down the rows peering and poking into lunch
10 containers, nodding if the contents pleased her, frowning a little at others. She stopped at Walter Cunningham's desk. 'Where's yours?' she asked.

Walter Cunningham's face told everybody in the first grade he had hookworms. His absence of shoes told us how he got them. People caught hookworms going bare-footed in barnyards and hog wallows. If Walter had owned any shoes he would have worn them the first day of school and then discarded them until mid-winter. He did have on a clean shirt and neatly mended overalls.
20 'Did you forget your lunch this morning?' asked Miss Caroline.

Walter looked straight ahead. I saw a muscle jump in his skinny jaw.

'Did you forget it this morning?' asked Miss Caroline. Walter's jaw twitched again.

'Yeb'm,' he finally mumbled.

Miss Caroline went to her desk and opened her purse. 'Here's a quarter,' she said to Walter. 'Go and eat downtown today. You can pay me back tomorrow.'

30   Walter shook his head. 'Nome thank you ma'am,' he drawled softly.

Impatience crept into Miss Caroline's voice: 'Here Walter, come get it.'

Walter shook his head again.

When Walter shook his head a third time someone whispered, 'Go on and tell her, Scout.'

I turned around and saw most of the town people and the entire bus delegation looking at me. Miss Caroline and I had conferred twice already, and they were looking
40   at me in the innocent assurance that familiarity breeds understanding.

I rose graciously on Walter's behalf: 'Ah – Miss Caroline?'

'What is it, Jean Louise?'

'Miss Caroline, he's a Cunningham.'

I sat back down.

'What, Jean Louise?'

I thought I had made things sufficiently clear. It was clear enough to the rest of us: Walter Cunningham was
50   sitting there lying his head off. He didn't forget his lunch, he didn't have any. He had none today nor would he have any tomorrow or the next day. He had probably never seen three quarters together at the same time in his life.

I tried again: 'Walter's one of the Cunninghams, Miss Caroline.'

'I beg your pardon, Jean Louise?'

'That's okay, ma'am, you'll get to know all the county folks after a while. The Cunninghams never took
60   anything they can't pay back – no church baskets and no scrip stamps. They never took anything off anybody,

they get along on what they have. They don't have much, but they get along on it.'

My special knowledge of the Cunningham tribe – one branch, that is – was gained from events of last winter. Walter's father was one of Atticus's clients. After a dreary conversation in our living-room one night about his entailment, before Mr Cunningham left he said, 'Mr Finch, I don't know when I'll ever be able to pay you.'

70 'Let that be the least of your worries, Walter,' Atticus said.

When I asked Jem what entailment was, and Jem described it as a condition of having your tail in a crack, I asked Atticus if Mr Cunningham would ever pay us.

'Not in money,' Atticus said, 'but before the year's out I'll have been paid. You watch.'

We watched. One morning Jem and I found a load of stove-wood in the back yard. Later, a sack of hickory nuts appeared on the back steps. With Christmas came

80 a crate of smilax and holly. That spring when we found a croker-sack full of turnip greens, Atticus said Mr Cunningham had more than paid him.

'Why does he pay you like that?' I asked.

'Because that's the only way he can pay me. He has no money.'

'Are we poor, Atticus?'

Atticus nodded. 'We are indeed.'

Jem's nose wrinkled. 'Are we as poor as the Cunninghams?'

90 'Not exactly. The Cunninghams are country folks, farmers, and the crash hit them hardest.'

Atticus said professional people were poor because the farmers were poor. As Maycomb County was farm country, nickels and dimes were hard to come by for doctors and dentists and lawyers. Entailment was only a part of Mr Cunningham's vexations. The acres not entailed were mortgaged to the hilt, and the little cash

100

he made went to interest. If he held his mouth right, Mr Cunningham could get a W. P. A. job, but his land would go to ruin if he left it, and he was willing to go hungry to keep his land and vote as he pleased. Mr Cunningham, said Atticus, came from a set breed of men.

110

As the Cunninghams had no money to pay a lawyer, they simply paid us with what they had. 'Did you know,' said Atticus, 'that Dr Reynolds works the same way? He charges some folks a bushel of potatoes for delivery of a baby. Miss Scout, if you give me your attention I'll tell you what entailment is. Jem's definitions are very nearly accurate sometimes.'

If I could have explained these things to Miss Caroline, I would have saved myself some inconvenience and Miss Caroline subsequent mortification, but it was beyond my ability to explain things as well as Atticus, so I said, 'You're shamin' him, Miss Caroline. Walter hasn't got a quarter at home to bring you, and you can't use any stovewood.'

120

Miss Caroline stood stock still, then grabbed me by the collar and hauled me back to her desk. 'Jean Louise, I've had about enough of you this morning,' she said. 'You're starting off on the wrong foot in every way, my dear. Hold out your hand.'

130

I thought she was going to spit in it, which was the only reason anybody in Maycomb held out his hand; it was a time-honoured method of sealing oral contracts. Wondering what bargain we had made, I turned to the class for an answer, but the class looked back at me in puzzlement. Miss Caroline picked up her ruler, gave me half a dozen quick little pats, then told me to stand in the corner. A storm of laughter broke loose when it finally occurred to the class that Miss Caroline had whipped me.

When Miss Caroline threatened it with a similar fate

the first grade exploded again, becoming cold sober only when the shadow of Miss Blount fell over them. Miss Blount, a native Maycombian as yet uninitiated in the mysteries of the Decimal System, appeared at the door hands on hips and announced: 'If I hear another sound from this room I'll burn up everybody in it. Miss Caroline, the sixth grade cannot concentrate on the pyramids for all this racket!'

My sojourn in the corner was a short one. Saved by the bell, Miss Caroline watched the class file out for lunch. As I was the last to leave, I saw her sink down into her chair and bury her head in her arms. Had her conduct been more friendly towards me, I would have felt sorry for her. She was a pretty little thing.

Harper Lee, *To Kill a Mockingbird* (1960)

Consider the way this episode is narrated. It has a double angle of vision that enables us to see the action through the eyes of the little girl, Scout, and also through the mature understanding and knowledge of the adult who recalls her childhood. These two perspectives on the events merge subtly together, contributing greatly to the warm humour of the novel and helping us to feel very much in sympathy with Scout as a little girl. She takes for granted many aspects of her society but with hindsight her adult self can present these matters coherently. For example, identify the humorous confusion that results from her inability to explain to Miss Caroline why it was inappropriate to give Walter Cunningham some money to buy lunch. Where else in this extract are you aware of Scout's naïvety?

Miss Caroline performs an important role because, as an outsider, unfamiliar with the ways of Maycomb, she causes a highlighting, an exposure of some of the qualities of its society that would otherwise remain unstated assumptions. Her blundering presence in the school creates a need for some explanation of the values and ways that the society of Maycomb County operates.

With these general points in mind, write an appreciation of the extract, bringing out the humour of the situation and your understanding of the social background of the people involved. The following questions may help you focus on particular aspects.

1 What do you learn about the life-pattern of the Cunninghams and about their sense of values? Consider the presentation of Walter Cunningham and Atticus's statement that Mr Cunningham 'came from a set breed of men' (lines 102–3).
2 What impression do you gain of Scout's home life? Consider the skill with which the author sets into the rest of the narrative the digression concerning the background to her understanding of the Cunninghams.
3 Identify those moments in which misunderstandings occur between Miss Caroline and the children and the effect these misunderstandings create for the reader. What assumptions govern her attitudes towards the children and how do the children see Miss Caroline?
4 What have you learnt of Maycombian society from this extract?

Outsider

In the society of Maycomb we appreciate a capacity for tolerance, flexibility and acceptance of people with divergent ways of life, though the novel as a whole contains far more than what might be superficially regarded as this sentimental view of human societies; exploitation of black people, intense colour prejudice, injustice, murder and revenge are all present. Nevertheless, the primary view is of a society that allows the individual to flourish, however non-conformist he may be, and the reason we condemn Miss Caroline is that she represents a *system*, an institutionalised approach to experience that takes no regard of the individual and is inflexible in its demands for absolute conformity. In this section of the chapter, however, we reverse the roles: it is the society that is repressive and it is the 'outsider' who stands for freedom and individuality.

Here is an extract from Aldous Huxley's *Brave New World*. It is a conversation between two men: Mustapha Mond, Resident Controller for Western Europe, one of the ten World Controllers in Huxley's futuristic society, and the Savage, accidentally born and raised in a savage reservation outside conventional society though not of savage parenthood. **A commentary and some background details to the passage follow it but before you read them, discuss or write about the extract, bringing out**:

1 what you learn about the way this *Brave New World* maintains its stability and how it deals with the feelings of individuals
2 the values the Savage wishes to assert.

'If you allowed yourselves to think of God, you wouldn't allow yourselves to be degraded by pleasant vices. You'd have a reason for bearing things patiently, for doing things with courage. I've seen it with the Indians.'

'I'm sure you have,' said Mustapha Mond. 'But then we aren't Indians. There isn't any need for a civilized man to bear anything that's seriously unpleasant. And as for doing things – Ford forbid that he should get the
10 idea into his head. It would upset the whole social order if men started doing things on their own.'

'What about self-denial, then? If you had a God, you'd have a reason for self-denial.'

'But industrial civilization is only possible when there's

no self-denial. Self-indulgence up to the very limits imposed by hygiene and economics. Otherwise the wheels stop turning.'

'You'd have a reason for chastity!' said the Savage, blushing a little as he spoke the words.

20 'But chastity means passion, chastity means neurasthenia. And passion and neurasthenia mean instability. And instability means the end of civilization. You can't have a lasting civilization without plenty of pleasant vices.'

'But God's the reason for everything noble and fine and heroic. If you had a God . . .'

'My dear young friend,' said Mustapha Mond, 'civilization has absolutely no need of nobility or heroism. These things are symptoms of political inefficiency. In a properly organized society like ours, nobody has any

30 opportunities for being noble or heroic. Conditions have got to be thoroughly unstable before the occasion can arise. Where there are wars, where there are divided allegiances, where there are temptations to be resisted, objects of love to be fought for or defended – there, obviously, nobility and heroism have some sense. But there aren't any wars nowadays. The greatest care is taken to prevent you from loving anyone too much. There's no such thing as a divided allegiance; you're so conditioned that you can't help doing what you ought to

40 do. And what you ought to do is on the whole so pleasant, so many of the natural impulses are allowed free play, that there really aren't any temptations to resist. And if ever, by some unlucky chance, anything unpleasant should somehow happen, why, there's always *soma* to give you a holiday from the facts. And there's always *soma* to calm your anger, to reconcile you to your enemies, to make you patient and long-suffering. In the past you could only accomplish these things by making a great effort and after years of hard moral training.

50 Now, you swallow two or three half-gramme tablets, and

there you are. Anybody can be virtuous now. You can carry at least half your morality about in a bottle. Christianity without tears – that's what *soma* is.'

'But the tears are necessary. Don't you remember what Othello said? "If after every tempest come such calms, may the winds blow till they have wakened death." There's a story one of the old Indians used to tell us, about the Girl of Mátsaki. The young men who wanted to marry her had to do a morning's hoeing in her garden. It seemed easy; but there were flies and mosquitoes, magic ones. Most of the young men simply couldn't stand the biting and stinging. But the one that could – he got the girl.'

'Charming! But in civilized countries,' said the Controller, 'you can have girls without hoeing for them; and there aren't any flies or mosquitoes to sting you. We got rid of them all centuries ago.'

The Savage nodded, frowning. 'You got rid of them. Yes, that's just like you. Getting rid of everything unpleasant instead of learning to put up with it. Whether 'tis nobler in the mind to suffer the slings and arrows of outrageous fortune, or to take arms against a sea of troubles and by opposing end them . . . . But you don't do either. Neither suffer nor oppose. You just abolish the slings and arrows. It's too easy.'

He was suddenly silent, thinking of his mother. In her room on the thirty-seventh floor, Linda had floated in a sea of singing lights and perfumed caresses – floated away, out of space, out of time, out of the prison of her memories, her habits, her aged and bloated body. And Tomakin, ex-Director of Hatcheries and Conditioning, Tomakin was still on holiday – on holiday from humiliation and pain, in a world where he could not hear those words, that derisive laughter, could not see that hideous face, feel those moist and flabby arms round his neck, in a beautiful world . . .

'What you need', the Savage went on, 'is something *with* tears for a change. Nothing costs enough here.'

90 ('Twelve and a half million dollars,' Henry Foster had protested when the Savage told him that. 'Twelve and a half million – that's what the new Conditioning Centre cost. Not a cent less.')

'Exposing what is mortal and unsure to all that fortune, death and danger dare, even for an egg-shell. Isn't there something in that?' he asked, looking up at Mustapha Mond. 'Quite apart from God – though of course God would be a reason for it. Isn't there something in living dangerously?'

'There's a great deal in it,' the Controller replied.
100 'Men and women must have their adrenals stimulated from time to time.'

'What?' questioned the Savage, uncomprehending.

'It's one of the conditions of perfect health. That's why we've made the V.P.S. treatments compulsory.'

'V.P.S.?'

'Violent Passion Surrogate. Regularly once a month. We flood the whole system with adrenalin. It's the complete physiological equivalent of fear and rage. All the tonic effects of murdering Desdemona and being
110 murdered by Othello, without any of the inconveniences.'

'But I like the inconveniences.'

'We don't,' said the Controller. 'We prefer to do things comfortably.'

'But I don't want comfort. I want God, I want poetry, I want real danger, I want freedom, I want goodness. I want sin.'

'In fact,' said Mustapha Mond, 'you're claiming the right to be unhappy.'

'All right, then,' said the Savage defiantly, 'I'm
120 claiming the right to be unhappy.'

'Not to mention the right to grow old and ugly and impotent; the right to have syphilis and cancer; the right to have too little to eat; the right to be lousy; the right to live in constant apprehension of what may happen tomorrow; the right to catch typhoid; the right to be tortured by unspeakable pains of every kind.'

There was a long silence.

'I claim them all,' said the Savage at last.

Mustapha Mond shrugged his shoulders. 'You're welcome,' he said.

130

Aldous Huxley, *Brave New World* (1932)

Mustapha Mond supports a 'consumer society', one bent on maximum consumption of luxury products: 'self-indulgence up to the limits imposed by hygiene and economics'. Keeping the wheels turning means, for him, keeping everyone employed earning the money that they will spend on the products that, in turn, provide employment. So, the cycle, the nightmare of the age of technology, is justified. Absolute stability has been achieved by a world revolution maintained by the conditioning of all people to deny any inner compulsion of the soul. Conditioning is imposed in this society partly by what we might call genetic engineering and partly by brainwashing. The family no longer exists – even to speak of it is regarded as bad taste – and test-tube babies, their capacities determined before birth, are produced in 'hatcheries' under entirely artificial circumstances. Children are brought up in public institutions, where, during sleep, loudspeakers repeat simple statements that condition their responses. As Mond says, 'You're so conditioned that you can't help doing what you ought to do' (lines 38–40). He also refers to *soma*, a drug that produces instant pleasure and escapist relaxation, and without which this society could not possibly function. Notice the glowing terms in which he describes its effects and notice also what he says about the sexual habits of his society and about V. P. S. Of course, the question we must ask when we consider this fictional society of the future is whether it is, in any real sense, a critique of our own society. Huxley wrote the book in the early thirties, before television, genetic engineering and drugs were quite the issues they are today and before public debates on promiscuity and violence on TV. The blurb on a recent edition of the novel states that 'his world of test-tube babies and "feelies" is uncomfortably closer today than it was when the book was published'. Do you agree? Is this an example of the novelist as profound critic of our society and values?

The Savage comes from a different background and, as an outsider, he can stand for every reader of this novel who regards his own personality as important. In this 'brave new world', no one reads imaginative literature and books have been almost entirely destroyed but the Savage, as a child, discovered a copy of Shakespeare and his language is consequently permeated with the phrases and ideas of the dramatist. (How many are you able to identify in the extract we have considered? Can you track down the context of the title of the novel?) He stands for ideals of nobility, self-sacrifice and love, for the suffering that makes life significant and enables the individual spirit to grow. As he thinks of his mother, Linda, who had returned with him to the 'civilised' world from which she had been accidentally excluded at the time of his birth, and whose aged frame had not long survived the transition, he muses over a death that denied her the chance to come to terms with her past, to suffer and to achieve a personal resolution of her inner conflicts. Her decline and death had been a mere floating 'in a sea of singing lights and perfumed caresses'. Look again at the way this conversation comes to its climax, with the Savage embracing his condition as 'outsider', in full knowledge of the inevitable suffering that such a claim to freedom, goodness and sin implies.

Isolation, suffering and the tension of conflicting impulses is the fate of many 'outsiders' in modern novels, for this is a common enough theme in this century. In a sense, we are all outsiders or would-be outsiders, at least in youth, for only thus may we sense our individuality and differentiate ourselves from a society that often appears to be imposing a uniform standard upon us without regard to our individual needs. In the case of the Savage, or John as he is called when not being viewed through the eyes of the 'civilised' world, a state of extreme tension develops as a result of falling in love with Lenina. She, conditioned to regard exclusive loving as improper and promiscuous indulgence in sex as the only good way to live, attempts to seduce him. He is horrified, both at his own lustful thoughts and at her encouragement of them and, at the same time, he is full of remorse for what he regards as his failure to love his mother, Linda. Permitted to leave London and establish himself in a sort of hermitage, he seeks to come to terms with his mourning and love.

This episode is taken from the final chapter of the novel. **Write a full appreciation, bringing out the way the events and situations embody what you now understand to be the themes of the novel. If you need help in developing your commentary, consult the checklist of points that follows the passage.**

The weather was breathlessly hot, there was thunder in the air. He had dug all the morning and was resting, stretched out along the floor. And suddenly the thought of Lenina was a real presence, naked and tangible, saying 'Sweet!' and 'Put your arms round me!' – in shoes and socks, perfumed. Impudent strumpet! But oh, oh, her arms round his neck, the lifting of her breasts, her mouth! Eternity was in our lips and eyes. Lenina . . . No, no, no, no! He sprang to his feet and, half naked as he
10   was, ran out of the house. At the edge of the heath stood a clump of hoary juniper bushes. He flung himself against them, he embraced, not the smooth body of his desires, but an armful of green spikes. Sharp, with a thousand points, they pricked him. He tried to think of

poor Linda, breathless and dumb, with her clutching hands and the unutterable terror in her eyes. Poor Linda whom he had sworn to remember. But it was still the presence of Lenina that haunted him. Lenina whom he had promised to forget. Even through the stab and sting
20 of the juniper needles, his wincing flesh was aware of her, unescapably real. 'Sweet, sweet . . . And if you wanted me too, why didn't you. . .'

The whip was hanging on a nail by the door, ready to hand against the arrival of reporters. In a frenzy the Savage ran back to the house, seized it, whirled it. The knotted cords bit into his flesh.

'Strumpet! Strumpet!' he shouted at every blow as though it were Lenina (and how frantically, without knowing it, he wished it were!), white, warm, scented,
30 infamous Lenina that he was flogging thus. 'Strumpet!' And then, in a voice of despair, 'Oh, Linda, forgive me. Forgive me, God! I'm bad. I'm wicked. I'm. . . No, no, you strumpet, you strumpet!'

From his carefully constructed hide in the wood three hundred metres away, Darwin Bonaparte, the Feely Corporation's most expert big-game photographer, had watched the whole proceedings. Patience and skill had been rewarded. He had spent three days sitting inside the bole of an artificial oak tree, three nights crawling on his
40 belly through the heather, hiding microphones in gorse bushes, burying wires in the soft grey sand. Seventy-two hours of profound discomfort. But now the great moment had come – the greatest, Darwin Bonaparte had time to reflect, as he moved among his instruments, the greatest since his taking of the famous all-howling stereoscopic feely of the gorillas' wedding. 'Splendid,' he said to himself, as the Savage started his astonishing performance. 'Splendid!' He kept his telescopic cameras carefully aimed – glued to their moving objective; clapped on a
50 higher power to get a close-up of the frantic and distorted

face (admirable!); switched over, for half a minute, to slow motion (an exquisitely comical effect, he promised himself); listened in, meanwhile, to the blows, the groans, the wild and raving words that were being recorded on the sound-track at the edge of his film, tried the effect of a little amplification (yes, that was decidedly better); was delighted to hear, in a momentary lull, the shrill singing of a lark; wished the Savage would turn round so that he could get a good close-up of the blood on his back – and almost instantly (what astonishing luck!) the accommodating fellow did turn round, and he was able to take a perfect close-up.

'Well, that was grand!' he said to himself when it was all over. 'Really grand!' He mopped his face. When they had put in the feely effects at the studio, it would be a wonderful film. Almost as good, thought Darwin Bonaparte, as the *Sperm Whale's Love-Life* – and that, by Ford, was saying a good deal!

Twelve days later *The Savage of Surrey* had been released and could be seen, heard, and felt in every first-class feely-palace in Western Europe.

The effect of Darwin Bonaparte's film was immediate and enormous. On the afternoon which followed the evening of its release, John's rustic solitude was suddenly broken by the arrival overhead of a great swarm of helicopters.

He was digging in his garden – digging, too, in his own mind, laboriously turning up the substance of his thought. Death – and he drove in his spade once, and again, and yet again. And all our yesterdays have lighted fools the way to dusty death. A convincing thunder rumbled through the words. He lifted another spadeful of earth. Why had Linda died? Why had she been allowed to become gradually less than human and at last . . . He shuddered. A good kissing carrion. He planted his foot on his spade and stamped it fiercely into the

tough ground. As flies to wanton boys are we to the gods;
they kill us for their sport. Thunder again; words that
proclaimed themselves true – truer somehow than truth
90   itself. And yet that same Gloucester had called them
ever-gentle gods. Besides, thy best of rest is sleep, and
that thou oft provok'st; yet grossly fear'st thy death
which is no more. No more than sleep. Sleep. Perchance
to dream. His spade struck against a stone; he stooped
to pick it up. For in that sleep of death, what
dreams . . .?

A humming overhead had become a roar; and
suddenly he was in shadow, there was something
between the sun and him. He looked up, startled, from
100 his digging, from his thoughts; looked up in dazzled
bewilderment, his mind still wandering in that other
world of truer-than-truth, still focused on the immensities
of death and deity; looked up and saw, close above him,
the swarm of hovering machines. Like locusts they came,
hung poised, descended all round him on the heather.
And from out of the bellies of these giant grasshoppers
stepped men in white viscose-flannels, women (for the
weather was hot) is acetate-shantung pyjamas or
velveteen shorts and sleeveless, half-unzippered singlets
110 – one couple from each. In a few minutes there were
dozens of them, standing in a wide circle round the lighthouse, staring, laughing, clicking their cameras, throwing
(as to an ape) pea-nuts, packets of sex-hormone chewing-
gun, pan-glandular *petits beurres*. And every moment – for
across the Hog's Back the stream of traffic now flowed
unceasingly – their numbers increased. As in a nightmare, the dozens became scores, the scores hundreds.

The Savage had retreated towards cover, and now, in
the posture of an animal at bay, stood with his back to
120 the wall of the lighthouse, staring from face to face in
speechless horror, like a man out of his senses.

Aldous Huxley, *Brave New World* (1932)

Below is a checklist of issues that should be raised in your commentary on the passage:

1   How the Savage's conflict of obligation and desire is expressed in his actions and words. Perhaps you can identify the part played by some of his Shakespearian utterances.

2   Appreciation of the way the 'big-game photographer' and his activities are described. How does he enable us to see the Savage in a different perspective? Is there humour in his presentation? in his name?

3   The nature of John's 'digging' (lines 77–96). How, again, is physical activity used to dramatise mental processes? Does his state of mind seem to have changed since the episode of the whipping?

4   The effectiveness of phrases like 'something between the sun and him' (lines 98–99) and of 'like locusts' (line 104).

5   How the invading horde is presented and how the quality of its culture is suggested.

At this point in the novel, we are within three pages of its conclusion. **Speculate as to how the events will progress and the probable end of the novel, or, better still, write your own version of its conclusion, bearing in mind the issues that you think will need resolution.**

Repression

Brave New World offers its people a life of painless nonentity; absence of tension, striving, unhappiness and personal trauma compensate for the loss of individuality. A very far cry from this seductive ease is George Orwell's vision of a future totalitarian state in *Nineteen Eighty-Four*. Life here is meagre and uncomfortable, a matter of service to the state without private feelings or thoughts. Telescreens in every room scan people's movements and behind the paraphernalia of perpetual spying lurks the Thought Police, exercising an extreme form of censorship in this totally repressive society.

The hero of *Nineteen Eighty-Four* is Winston Smith, middle-aged, battered and ordinary in all respects apart from his secret retention of a hope that there may exist a secret brotherhood through which society might be undermined. As he pursues his solitary life in the early part of the novel he becomes convinced that a girl, who works in the same building as he, is an agent of the Thought Police and is spying on him.

This extract comes from the opening of Part 2 of the novel, in which significant new developments occur in Winston's life. **Write an appreciation of it, using these questions to help you focus on its significant details.**

1 Which background details help you to grasp the attitude of this society towards the individual? How does Orwell convey the continuous and immediate control of the state over Winston?

2 Notice the sequence of Winston's thoughts and feelings. At which moments does he suppress his natural feelings and where does his instinct take over? Define the conflicts he experiences.

3 Which details suggest the personalities and habitual responses of these two people? Do they seem 'normal' in their responses or has their society induced an unbalanced development of characteristics?

4 Describe the style of the extract. Has it any relationship with the quality of life that Orwell presents?

It was the middle of the morning, and Winston had left the cubicle to go to the lavatory.

A solitary figure was coming towards him from the other end of the long, brightly-lit corridor. It was the girl with dark hair. Four days had gone past since the evening when he had run into her outside the junk-shop. As she came nearer he saw that her right arm was in a sling, not noticeable at a distance because it was of the same colour as her overalls. Probably she had crushed her hand while swinging round one of the big kaleidoscopes on which the plots of novels were 'roughed in'. It was a common accident in the Fiction Department.

They were perhaps four metres apart when the girl stumbled and fell almost flat on her face. A sharp cry of pain was wrung out of her. She must have fallen right on the injured arm. Winston stopped short. The girl had risen to her knees. Her face had turned a milky yellow colour against which her mouth stood out redder than ever. Her eyes were fixed on his, with an appealing expression that looked more like fear than pain.

A curious emotion stirred in Winston's heart. In front of him was an enemy who was trying to kill him: in front of him, also, was a human creature, in pain and perhaps with a broken bone. Already he had instinctively started forward to help her. In the moment when he had seen her fall on the bandaged arm, it had been as though he felt the pain in his own body.

'You're hurt?' he said.

'It's nothing. My arm. It'll be all right in a second.' She spoke as though her heart were fluttering. She had certainly turned very pale.

'You haven't broken anything?'

'No, I'm all right. It hurt for a moment, that's all.' She held out her free hand to him, and he helped her up. She had regained some of her colour, and appeared very much better.

'It's nothing,' she repeated shortly. 'I only gave my wrist a bit of a bang. Thanks, comrade!'

And with that she walked on in the direction in which she had been going, as briskly as though it had really been nothing. The whole incident could not have taken as much as half a minute. Not to let one's feelings appear in one's face was a habit that had acquired the status of an instinct, and in any case they had been standing straight in front of a telescreen when the thing happened. Nevertheless it had been very difficult not to betray a momentary surprise, for in the two or three seconds while he was helping her up the girl had slipped something into his hand. There was no question that she had done it intentionally. It was something small and flat. As he passed through the lavatory door he transferred it to his pocket and felt it with the tips of his fingers. It was a scrap of paper folded into a square.

While he stood at the urinal he managed, with a little more fingering, to get it unfolded. Obviously there must be a message of some kind written on it. For a moment he was tempted to take it into one of the water-closets and read it at once. But that would be shocking folly, as he well knew. There was no place where you could be more certain that the telescreens were watched continuously.

He went back to his cubicle, sat down, threw the fragment of paper casually among the other papers on the desk, put on his spectacles and hitched the speakwrite towards him. 'Five minutes,' he told himself, 'five minutes at the very least!' His heart bumped in his breast with frightening loudness. Fortunately the piece of work he was engaged on was mere routine, the rectification of a long list of figures, not needing close attention.

Whatever was written on the paper, it must have some kind of political meaning. So far as he could see there were two possibilities. One, much the more likely, was that the girl was an agent of the Thought Police, just as he had feared. He did not know why the Thought Police should choose to deliver their messages in such a fashion, but perhaps they had their reasons. The thing that was written on the paper might be a threat, a summons, an

order to commit suicide, a trap of some description. But there was another, wilder possibility that kept raising its
80 head, though he tried vainly to suppress it. This was, that the message did not come from the Thought Police at all, but from some kind of underground organization. Perhaps the Brotherhood existed after all! Perhaps the girl was part of it! No doubt the idea was absurd, but it had sprung into his mind in the very instant of feeling the scrap of paper in his hand. It was not till a couple of minutes later that the other, more probable explanation had occurred to him. And even now, though his intellect told him that the message probably meant death
90 – still, that was not what he believed, and the unreasonable hope persisted, and his heart banged, and it was with difficulty that he kept his voice from trembling as he murmured his figures into the speakwrite.

He rolled up the completed bundle of work and slid it into the pneumatic tube. Eight minutes had gone by. He re-adjusted his spectacles on his nose, sighed, and drew the next batch of work towards him, with the scrap of paper on top of it. He flatttened it out. On it was written, in a large unformed handwriting:

100 *I love you.*

For several seconds he was too stunned even to throw the incriminating thing into the memory hole. When he did so, although he knew very well the danger of showing too much interest, he could not resist reading it once again, just to make sure that the words were really there.

George Orwell, *Nineteen Eighty-Four* (1949)

This is an uncomfortable passage to read; the impoverished, meagre quality of personal life in the totalitarian state comes across most strongly. Consider the bleak style, unadorned with metaphor or image: the opening paragraph with its bald, matter-of-fact realism is typical. It is on the way to the lavatory, in a 'long, brightly-lit corridor', in impersonal, almost sordid circumstances that a declaration of love is made. Compare the style with that of *Brave New World*: there is nothing of the wit or humour related to the 'big-game photographer', Darwin Bonaparte, with his mock-heroic name, or which results from the contrast between the Savage's use of language with all its elevated Shakespearian phrasing and the empty clichés of the people around him. Here, in *Nineteen Eighty-Four*, is a uniform banality of statement, flat and clear, in its way a precise style with its feet always firmly on the ground. Notice, for example, how the girl's appearance is described: 'Her face had turned a milky yellow colour against which her mouth stared out redder then ever.' It is not an attractive vision; yellow milk has unwholesome connotations and her face is like that of a doll or a clown. Winston sees mere colours, a sort of mask, not the expressive countenance of another human being, someone with whom, he is going to fall in love.

So the style perfectly mirrors the emotional deprivations of the characters. Winston gives flat, blandly rational explanations of things he notices. How, for example, does he explain the presence of the girl's sling? Look again at the thoughts he has about the piece of paper she has pressed into his hand. Is it not significant that in his careful speculation over the contents of what he deduces must be a note, he does not consider the possibility of its being a personal message? The other, more obvious ways in which both Winston and the girl are inhibited in their capacity to feel and express themselves will have occurred to you as you wrote about the passage but notice the feelings described in the fourth paragraph. Why is it so apt, in these circumstances, to call Winston's response a 'curious emotion'? What is left when true feelings are inhibited? Only caution and self-protection and fear. It is fear that dominates the passage and communicates its tension to us: fear of self-revelation, fear of the girl, of discovery, of having private feelings and of showing those feelings in public.

Can the individual survive in such a society? The question remains open during the first and second sections of the novel, but in Part 3 the answer becomes all too clear. Winston and the girl, Julia, fall in love and are allowed to enjoy some measure of private life but at all times they are being watched by the Thought Police. Part 3 brings Winston to an experience of interrogation and torture that alters his responses finally and irrevocably. Towards the end of the novel, they meet again. **Write an appreciation of this description of their meeting, making reference to the first extract if it helps.**

Actually it was by chance that they had met. It was in the Park, on a vile, biting day in March, when the earth was like iron and all the grass seemed dead and there was not a bud anywhere except a few crocuses which had pushed themselves up to be dismembered by the wind. He was hurrying along with frozen hands and watering eyes when he saw her not ten metres away from him. It struck him at once that she had changed in some ill-defined way. They almost passed one another without
10 a sign, then he turned and followed her, not very eagerly. He knew that there was no danger, nobody would take any interest in them. She did not speak. She walked obliquely away across the grass as though trying to get rid of him, then seemed to resign herself to having him at her side. Presently they were in among a clump of ragged leafless shrubs, useless either for concealment or as protection from the wind. They halted. It was vilely cold. The wind whistled through the twigs and fretted the occasional, dirty-looking crocuses. He put his arm
20 round her waist.

There was no telescreen, but there must be hidden

microphones: besides, they could be seen. It did not matter, nothing mattered. They could have lain down on the ground and done *that* if they had wanted to. His flesh froze with horror at the thought of it. She made no response whatever to the clasp of his arm; she did not even try to disengage herself. He knew now what had changed in her. Her face was sallower, and there was a long scar, partly hidden by the hair, across her forehead
30 and temple; but that was not the change. It was that her waist had grown thicker, and, in a surprising way, had stiffened. He remembered how once, after the explosion of a rocket bomb, he had helped to drag a corpse out of some ruins, and had been astonished not only by the incredible weight of the thing, but by its rigidity and awkwardness to handle, which made it seem more like stone than flesh. Her body felt like that. It occurred to him that the texture of her skin would be quite different from what it had once been.

40 He did not attempt to kiss her, nor did they speak. As they walked back across the grass she looked directly at him for the first time. It was only a momentary glance, full of contempt and dislike. He wondered whether it was a dislike that came purely out of the past or whether it was inspired also by his bloated face and the water that the wind kept squeezing from his eyes. They sat down on two iron chairs, side by side but not too close together. He saw that she was about to speak. She moved her clumsy shoe a few centimetres and deliberately
50 crushed a twig. Her feet seemed to have grown broader, he noticed.

'I betrayed you,' she said baldly.

'I betrayed you,' he said.

She gave him another quick look of dislike.

'Sometimes,' she said, 'they threaten you with something – something you can't stand up to, can't even think about. And then you say, "Don't do it to me, do it to

somebody else, do it to So-and-so." And perhaps you might pretend, afterwards, that it was only a trick and
60 that you just said it to make them stop and didn't really mean it. But that isn't true. At the time when it happens you do mean it. You think there's no other way of saving yourself, and you're quite ready to save yourself that way. You *want* it to happen to the other person. You don't give a damn what they suffer. All you care about is yourself.'

'All you care about is yourself,' he echoed.

'And after that, you don't feel the same towards the other person any longer.'

70 'No,' he said, 'you don't feel the same.'

There did not seem to be anything more to say. The wind plastered their thin overalls against their bodies. Almost at once it became embarrassing to sit there in silence: besides, it was too cold to keep still. She said something about catching her Tube and stood up to go.

'We must meet again,' he said.

'Yes,' she said, 'we must meet again.'

George Orwell, *Nineteen Eighty-Four* (1949)

3 Couples

There must be very few novels or short stories that do not involve the plotting and exploration of the interactions between people. We bring to the understanding of these fictional relationships precisely the same skills of response, intuition and analysis that we may exercise in real life on the close relationships that we have and which we observe around us. In this chapter we shall consider the ways in which emotionally involved couples have been presented in a few novels and, in examining the extracts, it may be helpful for you to ask yourself these two questions:

1 What appears to be the basis for the relationship? Does it include physical desire or circumstantial need, or is emotional need more evident or a kind of spiritual longing that finds expression through love?
2 What are the reasons for its success or failure? How capable are the partners of communicating and being aware of each other's needs? Does either depend overmuch on the other? Are they of contrasted or complementary personality?

The mere fact that we ask such questions about committed relationships such as marriage implies an attitude that is both more intense and more questing than operated in some ages and which indeed operates now in some cultures. We are less bound by the social forms that have demanded arranged marriages and a prescribed code of behaviour between individuals. In those circumstances, when the maintaining of relationships for social reasons was of primary importance, then the values associated with them were those of discipline, self-restraint and the capacity of the partners to make the best of a bad job, if it were necessary. But because we tend to see personal growth as of greater importance than the maintenance of social forms, our views of relationships are more fluid and uncertain. Just as novelists have been aware of the need for a society to be sufficiently liberal for the individual to reach personal maturity, so they have explored ways in which relationships may be ennobling and liberating or constricting.

However, as literary critics, we are not psychologists, though psychological insight is part of our armoury, and we must also respond to the style of the writing we are considering. As you evaluate what you encounter of human relationships in this chapter, you must also be aware of how the novelist portrays them, what resources of language, of imagery, descriptive detail and symbolic suggestions are in evidence. A further group of questions might, therefore, be:

3 How does the novelist convey the qualities of this relationship to us? What is the relative importance of dialogue as against description of appearances and surroundings? Does the narrator explain the characters to us? How are sentences and paragraphs constructed? Is there anything significant about the language or imagery the author employs?

Expectations

Here is a nineteenth-century writer, a woman, herself something of a feminist whose own unconventional life resulted in her being ostracised by much of Victorian society. In her great novel, *Middlemarch*, George Eliot introduces an idealistic and impressionable young woman called Dorothea and a middle-aged bachelor, Mr Casaubon, who is engaged in a laborious and, it is implied, futile work of research entitled *The Key to All Mythologies*. The pair are shortly to be married and George Eliot describes them as they anticipate marriage and as they discuss their honeymoon arrangements.

Poor Mr. Casaubon had imagined that his long, studious bachelorhood had stored up for him a compound interest of enjoyment and that large drafts on his affections would not fail to be honoured; for we all of us, grave or light, get our thoughts entangled in metaphors and act fatally on the strength of them. And now he was in danger of being saddened by the very conviction that his circumstances were unusually happy: there was nothing external by which he could account for a certain blankness of sensibility which came over him just when his expectant gladness should have been most lively, just when he exchanged the accustomed dulness of his Lowick library for his visits to the Grange. Here was a weary experience in which he was as utterly condemned to loneliness as in the despair which sometimes threatened him while toiling in the morass of authorship without seeming nearer to the goal. And his was that worst loneliness which would shrink from sympathy. He could not but wish that Dorothea should think him not less happy than the world would expect her successful suitor to be; and in relation to his authorship he leaned on her young trust and veneration, he liked to draw forth her fresh interest in listening as a means of encouragement to himself: in talking to her he presented all his performance and intention with the reflected confidence of the pedagogue and rid himself for the time of that chilling ideal audience which crowded his laborious uncreative hours with the vaporous pressure of Tartarean shades.

For to Dorothea, after that toy-box history of the world adapted to young ladies which had made the chief part of her education, Mr. Casaubon's talk about his great book was full of new vistas; and this sense of revelation, this surprise of a nearer introduction to Stoics and Alexandrians as people who had ideas not totally unlike her own, kept in abeyance for the time her usual eagerness for a binding theory which could bring her own life and doctrine into strict connexion with that amazing past and give the remotest sources of knowledge some bearing on her actions. That more complete teaching would come – Mr. Casaubon would tell her all that; she was looking forward to higher initiation in ideas, as she was looking forward to marriage, and blending her dim conceptions of both. It would be a great mistake to suppose that Dorothea would have cared about any share in Mr. Casaubon's learning as mere accomplishment; for though opinion in the neighbourhood of Freshitt and Tipton had pronounced her clever, that epithet would not have described her to circles in whose more precise vocabulary cleverness implies mere aptitude for knowing and doing, apart from character. All her eagerness for acquirement lay within that full current of sympathetic motive in which her ideas and impulses were habitually swept along. She did not want to deck herself with knowledge, to wear it loose from the nerves and blood that fed her action; and if she had written a book she must have done it as Saint Theresa did, under the command of an authority that constrained her conscience. But something she yearned for by which her life might be filled with action at once rational and ardent; and since the time was gone by for guiding visions and spiritual directors, since prayer heightened yearning but not instruction, what lamp was there but knowledge? Surely learned men kept the only oil, and who more learned than Mr. Casaubon?

Thus in these brief weeks Dorothea's joyous, grateful expectation was unbroken, and however her lover might occasionally be conscious of flatness, he could never refer it to any slackening of her affectionate interest.

The season was mild enough to encourage the project of extending the wedding journey as far as Rome, and Mr. Casaubon was anxious for this because he wished to inspect some manuscripts in the Vatican.

'I still regret that your sister is not to accompany us,' he said one morning, some time after it had been ascertained that Celia objected to go and that Dorothea did not wish for her companionship. 'You will have many lonely hours, Dorothea, for I shall be constrained to make the utmost use of my time during our stay in Rome, and I should feel more at liberty if you had a 80 companion.'

The words 'I should feel more at liberty' grated on Dorothea. For the first time in speaking to Mr. Casaubon she coloured from annoyance.

'You must have misunderstood me very much,' she said, 'if you think I should not enter into the value of your time, if you think that I should not willingly give up whatever interfered with your using it to the best purpose.'

'That is very amiable in you, my dear Dorothea,' said 90 Mr. Casaubon, not in the least noticing that she was hurt; 'but if you had a lady as your companion, I could put you both under the care of a cicerone, and we could thus achieve two purposes in the same space of time.'

'I beg you will not refer to this again,' said Dorothea rather haughtily. But immediately she feared that she was wrong, and turning towards him she laid her hand on his, adding in a different tone, 'Pray do not be anxious about me. I shall have so much to think of when I am alone. And Tantripp will be a sufficient companion, just 100 to take care of me. I could not bear to have Celia; she would be miserable.'

It was time to dress. There was to be a dinner-party that day, the last of the parties which were held at the Grange as proper preliminaries to the wedding, and Dorothea was glad of a reason for moving away at once on the sound of the bell, as if she needed more than her usual amount of preparation. She was ashamed of being irritated from some cause she could not define even to

herself; for though she had no intention to be untruthful,
110 her reply had not touched the real hurt within her. Mr.
Casaubon's words had been quite reasonable, yet they
had brought a vague instantaneous sense of aloofness on
his part.

'Surely I am in a strangely selfish, weak state of mind,'
she said to herself. 'How can I have a husband who is
so much above me without knowing that he needs me
less than I need him?'

George Eliot, *Middlemarch* (1872)

**Before you write about this passage, you need to work
through it carefully, weighing the implications of each
statement**. These comments and questions may help you.

1 In the first paragraph, consider the implications of the
metaphor by which Mr Casaubon measures the life of the
emotions. What is the author's attitude towards him? Her
comments on 'all of us, grave or light' (lines 4–5) imply that
she sets herself up as one who knows her characters,
explains them to us and, indeed, judges them. What is the
state of mind she reveals in Mr Casaubon as she describes
his visits to Dorothea at the Grange during their engagement? In what sense is he 'poor' (line 1)? What does
George Eliot think of his authorship if she describes it as
a 'morass' (line 16)? What impression are you given of his
courtship of Dorothea and what particular satisfaction does
he seem to have gained from his relationship with her? We
are told in the last statement of the first paragraph that,
when with Dorothea, he 'rid himself for the time of that
chilling ideal audience which crowded his laborious
uncreative hours with the vaporous pressure of Tartarean
shades'. What do you understand this statement to mean?

2 In the second paragraph, we learn of Dorothea's state of
mind and feelings about this relationship. Consider the

51

implications of George Eliot's referring to her education as a 'toy-box history of the world' (line 30) and also whether Dorothea's desire for knowledge is in some sense suspect, or criticised by the author. Why should she desire teaching that would 'give the remotest sources of knowledge some bearing on her actions' (lines 39–40)? What do we learn in this paragraph of her attitudes towards personal and social attainment? What did Mr Casaubon seem to offer her?

3 As you respond to the passage of conversation, identify the moments of misunderstanding and of failure to communicate. Do you find yourself saddened or irritated by anything in their dialogue? What exactly is 'the hurt' (line 110) that Dorothea has felt? Why is she unable to define it even to herself (line 108) and unwilling to communicate her uncertainty to Mr Casaubon? How do you react to her final statement in this extract? Try to sum up what further insights into the nature of this relationship are offered in this conversation and Dorothea's thoughts after it. To what extent does Mr Casaubon understand Dorothea or she him? Is either of them 'using' the other? What are the prospects here for a successful marriage? In which areas of their experience are they likely to be able to communicate?

4 Finally, ask yourself whether you feel more sympathy towards one character than towards the other and whether this derives from a biased presentation by the author.

Now write a critical appreciation of the way this relationship is presented to us in this extract.

Separation

Thomas Hardy's novels are much concerned with the disruptive effect that differences in social status or changes within the rural world may have on close relationships. *The Woodlanders* is set in a remote part of the west of England in the late nineteenth century. Grace Melbury returns home from her finishing school and, encouraged by her father's social aspirations, becomes unwilling to continue the relationship she previously had with Giles Winterborne, a good but unsophisticated countryman. Instead she marries Fitzpiers, a doctor who had recently moved into the area. In the final stage of their honeymoon, Grace and Fitzpiers stay in an inn where, by coincidence, Giles has set up his cider press.

The chief hotel at Sherton Abbas was the 'Earl of Wessex' – a large stone-fronted inn with a yawning arch under which vehicles were driven by stooping coachmen to back premises of wonderful commodiousness. The windows to the street were mullioned into narrow lights, and only commanded a view of the opposite house; hence, perhaps, it arose that the best and most luxurious private sitting-room that the inn could afford overlooked the lateral parts of the establishment, where beyond the
10 yard were to be seen gardens and orchards now bossed, nay encrusted, with scarlet and gold fruit, stretching to infinite distance under a luminous lavender mist. The time was early autumn,

'When the fair apples, red as evening sky,
Do bend the tree unto the fruitful ground,
When juicy pears, and berries of black dye
Do dance in air, and call the eyes around.'

The landscape confronting the window might indeed have been part of the identical stretch of country which
20 the youthful Chatterton had in his mind when he penned those lines.

In this room sat she who had been the maiden Grace Melbury till the finger of fate touched her and turned her to a wife. It was two months after the wedding, and she was alone. Fitzpiers had walked out to see the abbey by

53

the light of sunset, but she had been too fatigued to accompany him. They had reached the last stage of a long eight-weeks' tour, and were going on to Hintock that night.

30   In the yard between Grace and the orchards there progressed a scene natural to the locality at this time of the year. An apple-mill and press had been erected on the spot, to which some men were bringing fruit from divers points in mawn-baskets, while others were grinding them, and others wringing down the pomace, whose sweet juice gushed forth into tubs and pails. The superintendent of these proceedings, to whom the others spoke as master, was a young yeoman of prepossessing manner and aspect, whose form she recognized in a

40   moment. He had hung his coat to a nail of the outhouse wall, and wore his shirt-sleeves rolled up beyond his elbows, to keep them unstained while he rammed the pomace into the bags of horsehair. Fragments of apple-rind had alighted upon the brim of his hat – probably from the bursting of a bag – while brown pips of the same fruit were sticking among the down upon his fine round arms, and in his beard.

Thomas Hardy, *The Woodlanders* (1887)

There is much insight into the true relationship between Grace and Giles to be gained from a close reading of these paragraphs, although the relationship as such is not directly treated in them. Grace is introduced as someone whom 'fate' has turned into a wife, deliberately 'touching' her. It is as if some transformation has occurred without her being aware of it, a magical, rather sinister, change. This sentence implies what the rest of the novel very clearly reveals, that in her marriage Grace has been a passive victim, not a girl who has actually followed the dictates of her heart. Moreover, she is alone: her husband is sightseeing but she is depleted of energy and remains in her room in the inn. The situation may suggest a disharmony between the couple, the weariness of a marriage that seems not to be proving satisfactory. Grace is, after all, a robust country girl for all her education and her fatigue is more likely to have emotional than physical origins.

In contrast with her lonely isolation in the grandest room of the inn is the scene of natural vigour, vitality and fruitfulness in the yard outside. The yard is actually closer to the orchards than Grace is and symbolically more identified with real growth and natural life. Notice how many details in this third paragraph suggest vigorous movement, strength and sweetness. The 'sweet juice' of the apples 'gushed forth into tubs and pails' (not 'dropped' or 'oozed') overflowing in its abundance and wholesomeness, and the men are all active, performing the various tasks of cider-making. The focus of these qualities is Giles Winterborne whose rolled-up shirt sleeves betoken the decorum and dress of civilisation giving way to more fundamental demands of rural life. His movements are described forcefully: 'he rammed the pomace into the bags of horsehair'. Even the stuff from which the bags are made carries associations of animal vigour and masculinity as do his 'fine round arms' and 'his beard'. The fragments of apple-rind and the brown pips of the fruit, suggesting new growth and renewal, have adhered to him. So, he is utterly identified with nature and the harvest, with strength and sweetness.

From all of this Grace is excluded, sitting passively and alone in the best room of the inn, but her separation is less real than her underlying understanding of the scene and her emotional identification with it. A little later we are told of the different apples she sees in the baskets and Hardy speculates about her thoughts:

. . . before the standard crop came in there accumulated, in abundant times like this, a large superfluity of early apples, and windfalls from the trees of later harvest, which would not keep long. Thus in the baskets, and quivering in the hopper of the mill, she saw specimens of mixed dates, including the mellow countenances of streaked-jacks, codlins, costards, stubbards, ratheripes, and other well-known friends of her ravenous youth.

Grace watched the head man with interest. The slightest sigh escaped her. Perhaps she thought of the day – not so far distant – when that friend of her childhood had met her by her father's arrangement in this same town, warm with hope, though diffident, and trusting in a promise rather implied than given. Or she might have thought of days earlier yet – days of childhood -- when her mouth was somewhat more ready to receive a kiss from his than was his to bestow one. However, all that was over. She had felt superior to him then, and she felt superior to him now.

Grace's knowledge of country tasks and of the varieties of apples suggests how much she is, at heart, a real part of this scene of harvest plenty, the reference to the 'well-known friends of her ravenous youth' reinforcing our sense that this is where she really belongs, this is where her roots are. In his speculation on her thoughts, Hardy draws out the ironies of the situation, how her relationship with Giles has changed, and he raises the question of why Grace allows 'the slightest sigh' to escape her. It must be the same motive that causes her, a moment or two later, to open the window and insist that Giles respond to her greeting, to the confusion and embarrassment of both of them.

Consider how Hardy's imaginative penetration of a complex human relationship extends to the way in which he creates situations and uses descriptive detail. This is a very different style from that of George Eliot where a clear, if very subtle, explanation of the relationship leads on to our experiencing the characters in dialogue with each other.

Later in *The Woodlanders*, Grace watches her husband set out, apparently to visit a sick patient. She believes that he is being unfaithful and, sure enough, from a distance she is able to see him riding the white horse, called Darling, which Giles had once given her, in an inappropriate direction, following a route which will take him to his mistress, Felice Charmond.

Write a full appreciation of this passage bringing out the significance of each descriptive detail.

Thus she had beheld the pet animal purchased for her own use, in pure love of her, by one who had always been true, impressed to convey her husband away from her to the side of a new-found idol. While she was musing on the vicissitudes of horses and wives, she discerned shapes moving up the valley towards her, quite near at hand, though till now hidden by the hedges. Surely they were Giles Winterborne, with two horses and a cider-apparatus, conducted by Robert Creedle. Up, upward they crept, a stray beam of the sun alighting every now and then like a star on the blades of the pomace-shovels, which had been converted to steel mirrors by the action of the malic acid. She descended to the road when he came close, and the panting horses rested as they achieved the ascent.

'How do you do, Giles?' said she, under a sudden impulse to be familiar with him.

He replied with much more reserve. 'You are going for a walk, Mrs. Fitzpiers?' he added. 'It is pleasant just now.'

'No, I am returning,' said she.

The vehicles passed on, and Creedle with them, and Winterborne walked by her side in the rear of the apple-mill.

He looked and smelt like Autumn's very brother, his
face being sunburnt to wheat-colour, his eyes blue as
corn-flowers, his sleeves and leggings dyed with fruit-
stains, his hands clammy with the sweet juice of apples,
his hat sprinkled with pips, and everywhere about him
that atmosphere of cider which at its first return each
season has such an indescribable fascination for those
who have been born and bred among the orchards. Her
heart rose from its late sadness like a released bough; her
senses revelled in the sudden lapse back to Nature
unadorned. The consciousness of having to be genteel
because of her husband's profession, the veneer of artificiality which she had acquired at the fashionable
schools, were thrown off, and she became the crude
country girl of her latent early instincts.

Nature was bountiful, she thought. No sooner had she
been cast aside by Edred Fitzpiers than another being,
impersonating chivalrous and undiluted manliness, had
arisen out of the earth ready to her hand. This, however,
was an excursion of the imagination which she did not
wish to encourage, and she said suddenly, to disguise
the confused regard which had followed her thoughts,
'Did you meet my husband?'

Winterborne, with some hesitation: 'Yes.'

'Where did you meet him?'

'Near Reveller's Inn. I come from Middleton Abbey;
I have been making there for the last week.'

'Haven't they a mill of their own?'

'Yes, but it's out of repair.'

'I think – I heard that Mrs. Charmond had gone there
to stay?'

'Yes, I have seen her at the windows once or twice.'

Grace waited an interval before she went on; 'Did Mr.
Fitzpiers take the way to Middleton?'

'Yes. . . . I met him on Darling.' As she did not reply,

60 he added with a gentler inflection, 'You know why the mare was called that?'

'O yes – of course,' she answered quickly.

With their minds on these things they had passed so far round the hill that the whole west sky was revealed. Between the broken clouds they could see far into the recesses of heaven as they mused and walked, the eye journeying on under a species of golden arcades, and past fiery obstructions, fancied cairns, logan-stones, stalactites and stalagmites of topaz. Deeper than this

70 their gaze passed thin flakes of incandescence, till it plunged into a bottomless medium of soft green fire.

Her abandonment to the seductive hour and scene after her sense of ill-usage, her revolt for the nonce against social law, her passionate desire for primitive life may have showed in her face. Winterborne was looking at her, his eyes lingering on a flower that she wore in her bosom. Almost with the abstraction of a somnambulist he stretched out his hand and gently caressed the flower.

She drew back. 'What are you doing, Giles Winter-

80 borne?' she exclaimed, with severe surprise.

The evident absence of all premeditation from the act, however, speedily led her to think that it was not necessary to stand upon her dignity here and now. 'You must bear in mind, Giles,' she said kindly, 'that we are not as we were; and some people might have said that what you did was taking a liberty.'

Thomas Hardy, *The Woodlanders* (1887)

Communion

D H Lawrence must occupy a prominent place in any consideration of relationships as presented in novels. He saw himself as 'the priest of love' mediating to Western man in the twentieth century a glimpse of the liberating power of sexuality and passionate loving. In *Sons and Lovers* he is primarily concerned with the emotional development of Paul Morel who struggles to detach himself from his intense involvement with his mother and to form a satisfying relationship, first with Miriam and, later, with Clara.

What do you learn of the relationship between Miriam and Paul from this extract? I suggest you discuss or write about it before reading the commentary which follows it. Here are some questions to help you focus your thoughts:

1 Why was it so necessary to Miriam for Paul to see the rose bush? In what terms does she anticipate the experience?
2 What feelings does Paul seem to have and how do they change throughout the passage?
3 How are the roses described? Are there any other details of description which seem to you to have deeper or symbolic meaning?
4 What other aspects of the style, such as vocabulary or sentence structure, seem important?

He followed her across the nibbled pasture in the dusk. There was a coolness in the wood, a scent of leaves, of honeysuckle, and a twilight. The two walked in silence. Night came wonderfully there, among the throng of dark-trunks. He looked round, expectant.

She wanted to show him a certain wild-rose bush she had discovered. She knew it was wonderful. And yet, till he had seen it, she felt it had not come into her soul. Only he could make it her own, immortal. She was
10 dissatisfied.

Dew was already on the paths. In the old-oak wood a mist was rising, and he hesitated, wondering whether one whiteness were a strand of fog or only campion-flowers pallid in a cloud.

By the time they came to the pine-trees Miriam was getting very eager and very intense. Her bush might be gone. She might not be able to find it; and she wanted it so much. Almost passionately she wanted to be with him when he stood before the flowers. They were going to have a communion together – something that thrilled her, something holy. He was walking beside her in silence. They were very near to each other. She trembled, and he listened, vaguely anxious.

Coming to the edge of the wood, they saw the sky in front, like mother-of-pearl, and the earth growing dark. Somewhere on the outermost branches of the pine-wood the honeysuckle was streaming scent.

'Where?' he asked.

'Down the middle path,' she murmured, quivering.

When they turned the corner of the path she stood still. In the wide walk between the pines, gazing rather frightened, she could distinguish nothing for some moments; the greying light robbed things of their colour. Then she saw her bush.

'Ah!' she cried, hastening forward.

It was very still. The tree was tall and straggling. It had thrown its briers over a hawthorn-bush, and its long streamers trailed thick right down to the grass, splashing the darkness everywhere with great split stars, pure white. In bosses of ivory and in large splashed stars the roses gleamed on the darkness of foliage and stems and grass. Paul and Miriam stood close together, silent, and watched. Point after point the steady roses shone out of them, seeming to kindle something in their souls. The dusk came like smoke around, and still did not put out the roses.

Paul looked into Miriam's eyes. She was pale and expectant with wonder, her lips were parted, and her dark eyes lay open to him. His look seemed to travel down into her. Her soul quivered. It was the communion

she wanted. He turned aside, as if pained. He turned to
the bush.

'They seems as if they walk like butterflies, and shake
themselves,' he said.

She looked at her roses. They were white, some
incurved and holy, others expanded in an ecstasy. The
tree was dark as a shadow. She lifted her hand impul-
sively to the flowers; she went forward and touched them
in worship.

60   'Let us go,' he said.

There was a cool scent of ivory roses – a white, virgin
scent. Something made him feel anxious and imprisoned.
The two walked in silence.

'Till Sunday,' he said quietly, and left her; and she
walked home slowly, feeling her soul satisfied with the
holiness of the night. He stumbled down the path. And
as soon as he was out of the wood, in the free open
meadow, where he could breathe, he started to run as
fast as he could. It was like a delicious delirium in his
70   veins.

D H Lawrence, Sons and Lovers (1913)

Throughout this passage we are aware of an intensity of
feeling. The responses of both characters are wrought up to
a high pitch and we are forced to appreciate what the experience means, and how it means very different things, to both
of them. To start with, we have description which suggests
expectancy: the sensuous richness of the coolness, the scents
of leaves and honeysuckle, the quality of the twilight and
absence of sound all help to conjure up for us the wonder that
Paul feels. His tentative uncertainty in this almost unreal,
magical landscape is well caught in his 'wondering whether
one whiteness were a strand of fog or only campion-flowers
pallid in a cloud' (lines 12–14). Here the ethereal and the physical
seem to merge uncertainly in those two alternatives. Paul is

'open', receptive to the wonder of this place, not needing to grab hold of any particular sensation or knowledge for himself.

In contrast, Miriam displays a single-minded intensity: she seeks a sort of completion within herself and this spiritual fulfilment is to be obtained by using Paul and possessing the rose bush. Notice the language Lawrence uses when identifying this hunger in Miriam: it is a 'communion', 'something holy'. The same words recur later in the passage and are reinforced in their cluster of religious, spiritualised associations by 'ecstasy' and 'worship'.

It is not surprising that Paul feels 'vaguely anxious' in the midst of all this spiritualised desire, for it is not an intensity that can call forth from him the wholesome expression of his masculinity. What Miriam wants ceases with the deep look into each other's eyes that follows their seeing of the rose bush. We are told: 'His look seemed to travel down into her. Her soul quivered. It was the communion she wanted' (lines 49–51). This 'penetration' is all in the mind, in feelings. It is sufficient for Miriam, an intensification of her virginity, but Paul turns aside 'as if pained'. This is an emasculating experience for him, one that imprisons him in virginity. Notice how the scent of the roses becomes symbolic: 'there was a cool scent of ivory roses – a white virgin scent' (lines 61–62). What associations might 'ivory' have? How can a scent be 'white' or, indeed, 'virgin'? No wonder Paul needs to fight against his anxiety and sense of imprisonment by having recourse to the warm ordinariness of his colloquial comment on the roses: 'They seems as if they walk like butterflies, and shake themselves' (lines 53–54). He chooses a metaphor which asserts the vitality, the real life of the roses, by relating them to physical creatures. And when he breaks away from Miriam, how is this reassertion of the physical world further expressed?

There are more points to be made about the passage. Perhaps you commented on the extraordinary way in which the roses are described in lines 37–46 and felt that here, in spite of the disharmony between the characters, was a unity of response that enabled them to experience the bush in sympathy with each other. Perhaps you also commented on the structure of the sentences and paragraphs and Lawrence's way of repeating ideas and phrases, constantly redefining as sharply as may be, his explanations and descriptions of emotional states in short, stabbing sentences. Look again at this technique, tracing the most important repetitions through the passage. However, our primary response to the passage must be in terms of the relationship between Paul and Miriam. How do you feel about their friendship? What does each give to the other? How do you think their relationship will develop?

There are many other passages in *Sons and Lovers* of equal power. Either find one yourself and write a critical appreciation of it or write on the following passage which describes a moment of consummation in the relationship between Paul and Clara, the other woman with whom he becomes involved. Concentrate on bringing out the precisely defined states of being of the characters and on the ways Lawrence uses description of details from the natural world to symbolise or define human experience.

She looked at the stars in the black water. They lay very white and staring. It was an agony to know he would leave her, but it was almost an agony to have him near her.

'And if you made a nice lot of money, what would you do?' she asked.

'Go somewhere in a pretty house near London with my mother.'

'I see.'

10   There was a long pause.

'I could still come and see you,' he said. 'I don't know. Don't ask me what I should do; I don't know.'

There was a silence. The stars shuddered and broke

upon the water. There came a breath of wind. He went
suddenly to her, and put his hand on her shoulder.

'Don't ask me anything about the future,' he said
miserably. 'I don't know anything. Be with me now, will
you, no matter what it is?'

And she took him in her arms. After all, she was a
married woman, and she had no right even to what he
gave her. He needed her badly. She had him in her arms,
and he was miserable. With her warmth she folded him
over, consoled him, loved him. She would let the
moment stand for itself.

After a moment he lifted his head as if he wanted to
speak.

'Clara,' he said, struggling.

She caught him passionately to her, pressed his head
down on her breast with her hand. She could not bear
the suffering in his voice. She was afraid in her soul. He
might have anything of her – anything; but she did not
want to *know*. She felt she could not bear it. She wanted
him to be soothed upon her – soothed. She stood clasping
him and caressing him, and he was something unknown
to her – something almost uncanny. She wanted to
soothe him into forgetfulness.

And soon the struggle went down in his soul, and he
forgot. But then Clara was not there for him, only a
woman, warm, something he loved and almost
worshipped, there in the dark. But it was not Clara, and
she submitted to him. The naked hunger and inevit-
ability of his loving her, something strong and blind and
ruthless in its primitiveness, made the hour almost
terrible to her. She knew how stark and alone he was,
and she felt it was great that he came to her; and she
took him simply because his need was bigger either than
her or him, and her soul was still within her. She did this
for him in his need, even if he left her, for she loved him.

All the while the peewits were screaming in the field.

50 When he came to, he wondered what was near his eyes, curving and strong with life in the dark, and what voice it was speaking. Then he realized it was the grass, and the peewit was calling. The warmth was Clara's breathing heaving. He lifted his head, and looked into her eyes. They were dark and shining and strange, life wild at the source staring into his life, stranger to him, yet meeting him; and he put his face down on her throat, afraid. What was she? A strong, strange, wild life, that breathed with his in the darkness through this hour. It

60 was all so much bigger than themselves that he was hushed. They had met, and included in their meeting the thrust of the manifold grass-stems, the cry of the peewit, the wheel of the stars.

When they stood up they saw other lovers stealing down the opposite hedge. It seemed natural they were there; the night contained them.

D H Lawrence, *Sons and Lovers* (1913)

4 Women

The presentation of women in novels, especially those of the nineteenth century, offers us a particular example of the relationship between society and the individual who has to live within it and yet seeks to find adequate expression for her own needs and desires. Until recent times women's destiny was thought to be almost exclusively that of marriage, and failure to marry was the fate most feared by the heroines of a certain class in novels of the nineteenth century, a fate which might reduce the woman to dependency on relatives or to seeking employment as a governess. As you consider these extracts from *Emma, Jane Eyre, Wuthering Heights*, and *The Mill on the Floss*, try to be aware not only of what one might call the thematic content, that is, the roles ascribed to women in these passages, but also of their variety of style and tone.

Irony

Consider the subtlety of human interaction in the following passage from Jane Austen's *Emma*. The situation is a conversation between three characters, Mrs Weston, Emma and Mr Knightley. The last is a bachelor, a neighbouring landowner and Emma's sister's brother-in-law, who has been Emma's friend for years, in spite of the difference in their ages, for she is herself a young and unmarried woman. Mrs Weston, her former governess, is now married to a local gentleman. Also mentioned in the passage is Jane Fairfax, a young woman living temporarily in Highbury with her grandmother and rather ridiculous aunt, Miss Bates, and it is about Jane's attachment to the vulgar and pretentious Mrs Elton, wife of the vicar, that they first talk. Emma does not care for Jane Fairfax but has voiced her wonder at Jane's encouragement of the attentions of the dreadful Mrs Elton. Mrs Weston replies:

'We cannot suppose that she has any great enjoyment at the Vicarage, my dear Emma – but it is better than being always at home. Her aunt is a good creature, but, as a constant companion, must be very tiresome. We must consider what Miss Fairfax quits, before we condemn her taste for what she goes to.'

'You are right, Mrs Weston,' said Mr Knightley warmly, 'Miss Fairfax is as capable as any of us of forming a just opinion of Mrs Elton. Could she have chosen with whom to associate, she would not have chosen her. But (with a reproachful smile at Emma) she receives attentions from Mrs Elton, which nobody else pays her.'

Emma felt that Mrs Weston was giving her a momentary glance; and she was herself struck by his warmth. With a faint blush, she presently replied,

'Such attentions as Mrs Elton's, I should have imagined, would rather disgust than gratify Miss Fairfax. Mrs Elton's invitations I should have imagined any thing but inviting.'

'I should not wonder,' said Mrs Weston, 'if Miss Fairfax were to have been drawn on beyond her own inclination, by her aunt's eagerness in accepting Mrs Elton's civilities for her. Poor Miss Bates may very likely have committed her niece and hurried her into a greater appearance of intimacy than her own good sense would have dictated, in spite of the very natural wish of a little change.'

Both felt rather anxious to hear him speak again; and after a few minutes silence, he said,

'Another thing must be taken into consideration too – Mrs Elton does not talk *to* Miss Fairfax as she speaks *of* her. We all know the difference between the pronouns he or she and thou, the plainest-spoken amongst us; we all feel the influence of a something beyond common civility in our personal intercourse with each other – a something more early implanted. We cannot give any body the disagreeable hints that we may have been very full of the hour before. We feel things differently. And besides the operation of this, as a general principle, you may be sure that Miss Fairfax awes Mrs Elton by her superiority both of mind and manner; and that face to face Mrs Elton treats her with all the respect which she has a claim to. Such a woman as Jane Fairfax probably never fell in Mrs Elton's way before – and no degree of vanity can prevent her acknowledging her own comparative littleness in action, if not in consciousness.'

'I know how highly you think of Jane Fairfax,' said Emma. Little Henry was in her thoughts, and a mixture of alarm and delicacy made her irresolute what else to say.

'Yes,' he replied, 'any body may know how highly I think of her.'

'And yet,' said Emma, beginning hastily and with an arch look, but soon stopping – it was better, however, to know the worst at once – she hurried on – 'And yet, perhaps, you may hardly be aware yourself how highly it is. The extent of your admiration may take you by surprize some day or other.'

Mr Knightley was hard at work upon the lower buttons of his thick leather gaiters, and either the exertion of getting them together, or some other cause, brought the colour into his face, as he answered,

'Oh! are you there? But you are miserably behind-hand. Mr Cole gave me a hint of it six weeks ago.'

He stopped. Emma felt her foot pressed by Mrs Weston, and did not herself know what to think. In a moment he went on –

70 'That will never be, however, I can assure you. Miss Fairfax, I dare say, would not have me if I were to ask her – and I am very sure I shall never ask her.'

Emma returned her friend's pressure with interest; and was pleased enough to exclaim,

'You are not vain, Mr Knightley. I will say that for you.'

He seemed hardly to hear her; he was thoughtful – and in a manner which shewed him not pleased, soon afterwards said,

80 'So you have been settling that I should marry Jane Fairfax.'

'No indeed I have not. You have scolded me too much for match-making, for me to presume to take such a liberty with you. What I said just now, meant nothing. One says those sort of things, of course, without any idea of a serious meaning. Oh! no, upon my word I have not the smallest wish for your marrying Jane Fairfax or Jane any body. You would not come in and sit with us in this comfortable way, if you were married.'

Mr Knightley was thoughtful again. The result of his reverie was, 'No, Emma, I do not think the extent of my admiration for her will ever take me by surprize. I never had a thought of her in that way, I assure you.' And soon afterwards, 'Jane Fairfax is a very charming young woman – but not even Jane Fairfax is perfect. She has a fault. She has not the open temper which a man would wish for in a wife.'

Emma could not but rejoice to hear that she had a fault. 'Well,' said she, 'and you soon silenced Mr Cole, I suppose?'

100 'Yes, very soon. He gave me a quiet hint; I told him he was mistaken; he asked my pardon and said no more. Cole does not want to be wiser or wittier than his neighbours.'

Jane Austen, *Emma* (1816)

It is not easy to respond to all the nuances of Jane Austen's writing and I suggest that you discuss or write about the passage with these questions in mind before you consider the commentary on it that follows the questions.

1 For what reason do you suppose that Mrs Weston gives Emma 'a momentary glance' (lines 14–15)? It must be connected with Mr Knightley's comment and the 'reproachful smile' (line 11) that he has directed at Emma.

2 Consider all the possible reasons for Emma's response to Mr Knightley's comment. Is she necessarily thinking the same as Mrs Weston? From what feelings might her 'faint blush' have arisen?

3 What sort of man does Mr Knightley seem to be? Take into account his views on the relationship likely to exist between Mrs Elton and Miss Fairfax (lines 31–47)

4 Emma's concern for 'Little Henry' (line 49) needs a footnote: her sister is married to Mr Knightley's younger brother and since, at present, Mr Knightley is unmarried, their eldest child, little Henry of course, stands to inherit Mr Knightley's considerable property. So, what do you suppose to be the real reason for Emma's enquiries into Mr Knightley's attachment to Jane Fairfax?

5 How does Jane Austen convey to us Mr Knightley's reactions to Emma's enquiries (lines 60–65)? How do you respond to her presenting us with alternative reasons for his colouring (lines 61–63)?

6 Why do you think Mrs Weston presses Emma's foot (lines 66–67)?

7 What does Emma understand by this pressure?

8 Why should Mr Knightley be 'not pleased' (line 77) by Emma's speculations?

9 Finally, consider the interaction between Emma and Mr Knightley in the last part of the extract. What does it appear to you that Knightley is trying to convey to her? How receptive is she?

71

Irony always implies more than it openly states and the difficulty that faces any reader of Jane Austen's novels is to perceive all that she implies about the feelings and relationships between her characters. The clues to the reality behind the appearance of the discourse are subtle and easily missed. Mr Knightley casts a reproachful smile at Emma because she has not been friendly with Jane Fairfax in spite of the latter's trying circumstances. Mrs Weston appears to sense the significance of Mr Knightley's smile and to be concerned with how Emma has received it but Emma seems unaware of the criticism: she was 'struck with his warmth' (line 15), the level of Mr Knightley's interest in Jane. Why? Does she herself wish to be the focus of his interest? That would certainly be suggested by her anxiety to 'hear him speak again' (line 29) and by her persistence in questioning him over the extent of his admiration for Jane. She is 'pleased' (line 73) when she learns that he would never ask Miss Fairfax to marry him and is delighted when he criticises Jane's character. She even remarks that his marrying 'Jane Fairfax or Jane any body' would take his company from them and that loss she would regret. Emma says more than she need and the nervous jocularity of this throw-away comment alerts us to feelings within her that are not yet disclosed.

Emma *rationalises* her concern with Mr Knightley's affections, that is, she gives herself a reason for being so interested in him and the reason she provides is her fond concern for the future fortunes of her little nephew. Later in the novel, when her love for Mr Knightley is recognised, we hear no more of little Henry's prospects! But, at this stage, Emma is unaware of her own heart. Lively, witty, open in discourse, she enjoys the sort of conversation which need not involve her in a commitment of feeling. Because she has only a partial knowledge of her own true feelings, she is unable to respond at the deepest level to the feelings of others. She misunderstands Mrs Weston's cautionary pressure of the foot, clearly a warning that she should not further embarrass Mr Knightley, and interprets it as, in our age, we might interpret a nudge.

Mr Knightley, on the other hand, speaks with discernment and with honesty, even at the expense of his own sense of ease. When the conversation, led by the woman he secretly loves, turns to his matrimonial inclinations, he is embarrassed and must take refuge in fiddling with his gaiters. There is a natural thoughtfulness as he struggles to sort out his feelings and to make utterances that, whilst socially acceptable, nevertheless do some justice to his true feelings. He cannot but regret that Emma should even consider his marrying anyone else and something of that disappointment emerges when he says, 'So you have been settling that I should marry Jane Fairfax.' His next reverie produces a comment on Jane which is also an oblique compliment to Emma: 'She has not the open temper which a man would wish for in a wife.' But it will take some further experiences of blunder, mortification and even suffering before Emma develops the self-understanding that will enable her to perceive the true feelings of Mr Knightley and of herself.

Here for you to write a critical appreciation is the culmination of the novel, where the courtship of Emma and Mr Knightley, unacknowledged throughout, rises to the surface at last. Three footnotes, mere points of information, follow the extract. Mr Knightley is speaking of Jane Fairfax's engagement with Frank Churchill. . .

'Frank Churchill is, indeed, the favourite of fortune. Every thing turns out for his good. He meets with a young woman at a watering-place, gains her affection, cannot even weary her by negligent treatment – and had he and all his family sought round the world for a perfect wife for him, they could not have found her superior. His aunt is in the way. His aunt dies. He has only to speak. His friends are eager to promote his happiness. He has used every body ill – and they are all delighted to forgive him. He is a fortunate man indeed!'

10

'You speak as if you envied him.'

'And I do envy him, Emma. In one respect he is the object of my envy.'

Emma could say no more. They seemed to be within half a sentence of Harriet,[1] and her immediate feeling was to avert the subject, if possible. She made her plan; she would speak of something totally different – the children in Brunswick Square;[2] and she only waited for breath to begin, when Mr Knightley startled her, by saying,

20

'You will not ask me what is the point of envy. You are determined, I see, to have no curiosity. You are wise – but *I* cannot be wise. Emma, I must tell what you will not ask, though I may wish it unsaid the next moment.'

'Oh! then, don't speak it, don't speak it,' she eagerly cried. 'Take a little time, consider, do not commit yourself.'

'Thank you,' said he, in an accent of deep mortification, and not another syllable followed.

30

Emma could not bear to give him pain. He was wishing to confide in her – perhaps to consult her; cost her what it would, she would listen. She might assist his resolution, or reconcile him to it; she might give just praise to Harriet, or, by representing to him his own independence, relieve him from that state of indecision, which must be more intolerable than any alternative to such a mind as his. They had reached the house.

'You are going in, I suppose,' said he.

'No' – replied Emma – quite confirmed by the

40

depressed manner in which he still spoke – 'I should like to take another turn. Mr Perry[3] is not gone.' And, after proceeding a few steps, she added – 'I stopped you ungraciously, just now, Mr Knightley, and, I am afraid, gave you pain. But if you have any wish to speak openly to me as a friend, or to ask my opinion of any thing that you may have in contemplation – as a friend, indeed, you may command me. I will hear whatever you like. I will tell you exactly what I think.'

'As a friend!' repeated Mr Knightley. 'Emma, that I fear is a word – No, I have no wish – Stay, yes, why should I hesitate? I have gone too far already for concealment. Emma. I accept your offer – Extraordinary as it may seem, I accept it, and refer myself to you as a friend. Tell me, then, have I no chance of ever succeeding?'

He stopped in his earnestness to look the question, and the expression of his eyes overpowered her.

'My dearest Emma,' said he, 'for dearest you will always be, whatever the event of this hour's conversation, my dearest, most beloved Emma – tell me at once. Say "No," if it is to be said.' She could really say nothing. 'You are silent,' he cried, with great animation; 'absolutely silent! at present I ask no more.'

Emma was almost ready to sink under the agitation of this moment. The dread of being awakened from the happiest dream, was perhaps the most prominent feeling.

Jane Austen, *Emma* (1816)

1 Harriet is a young woman of obscure parentage whom Emma has patronised. Emma thinks Mr Knightley may be in love with Harriet.
2 'the children in Brunswick Square' are the children of Mr Knightley's brother and Emma's sister.
3 Mr Perry is the local doctor who is visiting Emma's valetudinarian father.

Atmosphere

We move from the secure social world of Jane Austen where, apart from material concerns, the primary tension is whether feelings of love will be strong enough to breach the inhibiting effects of social decorum, to a much wilder and more instinctive vision in the novels of the Brontë sisters. Charlotte Brontë's *Jane Eyre* follows the fortunes of its heroine from her sad, lonely childhood, an unloved orphan, brought up unwillingly in a wealthy household, sent out as a teacher and finding employment at Thornfield Hall where she is wooed by its owner, Mr Rochester.

This episode occurs on the evening prior to Jane's intended marriage with Mr Rochester. **Discuss or write about it with the following issues in mind**:

1 Jane's state of mind as she approaches her wedding day
2 those elements which create mystery or unease
3 the importance of the setting, the surroundings and the weather
4 the effect of the autobiographical narrative method.

The month of courtship had wasted: its very last hours were being numbered. There was no putting off the day that advanced – the bridal day; and all preparations for its arrival were complete. *I*, at least, had nothing more to do: there were my trunks, packed, locked, corded, ranged in a row along the wall of my little chamber: tomorrow, at this time, they would be far on their road to London: and so should I (D. V.), – or rather, not I, but one Jane Rochester, a person whom as yet I knew not.

10 The cards of address alone remained to mail on: they lay, four little squares, on the drawer. Mr. Rochester had himself written the direction, 'Mrs. Rochester, —— Hotel, London,' on each: I could not persuade myself to affix them, or to have them affixed. Mrs. Rochester! She did not exist: she would not be born till to-morrow, some time after eight o'clock A. M.; and I would wait to be assured she had come into the world alive before I assigned to her all that property. It was enough that in yonder closet, opposite my dressing-table, garments said

20 to be hers had already displaced my black stuff Lowood

frock and straw bonnet: for not to me appertained that suit of wedding raiment, the pearl-coloured robe, the vapoury veil, pendent from the usurped portmanteau. I shut the closet, to conceal the strange, wraith-like apparel it contained; which, at this evening hour – nine o'clock – gave out certainly a most ghostly shimmer through the shadow of my apartment. 'I will leave you by yourself, white dream,' I said. 'I am feverish: I hear the wind blowing: I will go out of doors and feel it.'

30 It was not only the hurry of preparation that made me feverish; not only the anticipation of the great change – the new life which was to commence tomorrow: both these circumstances had their share, doubtless, in producing that restless, excited mood which hurried me forth at this late hour into the darkening grounds; but a third cause influenced my mind more than they.

I had at heart a strange and anxious thought. Something had happened which I could not comprehend; no one knew of or had seen the event but myself: it had
40 taken place the preceding night. Mr. Rochester that night was absent from home; nor was he yet returned: business had called him to a small estate of two or three farms he possessed thirty miles off – business it was requisite he should settle in person, previously to his meditated departure from England. I waited now his return; eager to disburthen my mind, and to seek of him the solution of the enigma that perplexed me. Stay till he comes, reader; and, when I disclose my secret to him, you shall share the confidence.

50 I sought the orchard: driven to its shelter by the wind, which all day had blown strong and full from the south; without, however, bringing a speck of rain. Instead of subsiding as night drew on, it seemed to augment its rush and deepen its roar: the trees blew steadfastly one way, never writhing round, and scarcely tossing back their boughs once in an hour; so continuous was the strain

bending their branchy heads northward – the clouds drifted from pole to pole, fast following, mass on mass: no glimpse of blue sky had been visible that July day.

It was not without a certain wild pleasure I ran before the wind delivering my trouble of mind to the measure-less air-torrent thundering through space. Descending the laurel-walk, I faced the wreck of the chestnut-tree; it stood up, black and riven: the trunk, split down the centre, gasped ghastly. The cloven halves were not broken from each other, for the firm base and strong roots kept them unsundered below; though community of vitality was destroyed – the sap could flow no more: their great boughs on each side were dead, and next winter's tempests would be sure to fell one or both to earth: as yet, however, they might be said to form one tree – a ruin, but an entire ruin.

' You did right to hold fast to each other,' I said: as if the monster splinters were living things, and could hear me. 'I think, scathed as you look, and charred and scorched, there must be a little sense of life in you yet; rising out of that adhesion at the faithful, honest roots: you will never have green leaves more – never more see birds making nests and singing idyls in your boughs; the time of pleasure and love is over with you; but you are not desolate: each of you has a comrade to sympathise with him in his decay.' As I looked up at them, the moon appeared momentarily in that part of the sky which filled their fissure; her disk was blood-red and half overcast; she seemed to throw on me one bewildered, dreary glance, and buried herself again instantly in the deep drift of cloud. The wind fell, for a second, round Thorn-field; but far away over wood and water, poured a wild, melancholy wail: it was sad to listen to, and I ran off again.

Charlotte Brontë, *Jane Eyre* (1847)

These bold effects yield themselves up more readily than do the ironic nuances of Jane Austen. The whole passage is full of mystery and suspense and you should have noticed details such as Jane's harbouring of an incomprehensible secret (lines 38–40) and the 'wraith-like apparel' (lines 24–25) of her marital wardrobe, suggesting the unreality of the future that appears to lie so attractively before her. Out of doors, the violent and persistent wind comes from the south, symbolically the place of warmth and sexual freedom; its effect is irresistible; even trees cannot stand up against it. What powerful force operates so implacably in the life of Jane Eyre, with such violence and potential danger? She is certainly in a state of intuitive sympathy with the wind as she runs before it (lines 60–62).

Mr Rochester had proposed to Jane whilst a great storm had been raging and, at the moment of his proposal, the great chestnut tree had been struck by lightning. In this extract, the tree adds a gloomy foreboding of the ruin of hopes, which is intensified and directed if we know the circumstances in which it was so destroyed. However, even if we have not that piece of information, the condition of the tree is powerfully suggestive and symbolic. Its sap can flow no more: it is as if its own vegetative life-force has been taken from it, leaving behind a comradeship, a 'faithful, honest' type of relationship, an asexual partnership, no longer related to the passionate urgencies of life. This symbol, in fact, takes us to the heart of the novel, to its central, almost unconscious, conflict between an acknowledgement of the passionate force of sexuality and deep fear or distrust of that force. Jane addresses the 'monster splinters' of the tree and projects on to them the best that she can conceive of in human relationships.

What effect did you find created in the last sentences of this extract? The intensely visual and atmospheric image of the blood-red moon that appears but for an instant between the cleft halves of the tree and the aural image of the momentary lull in the wind that allows Jane to hear 'a wild melancholy wail' from the more distant storm, combine together to create an extraordinarily foreboding and fantastic background for the eve of her marriage. We might call the effect 'romantic' or 'gothic': it is a combination of strange extremes of perception, of the individual pursuing her life amongst forces she does not understand and cannot control.

Finally, you will have commented on the contribution of the autobiographical narrative stance which is most clearly evident in lines 47–49. The style of the narration is careful, ordered, a slow and wholly conscious unfolding of the sequence of events, of the mysteries. Note the precise and judicious statement of alternatives in the second paragraph and the almost banal and laborious manner in which Jane addresses the riven tree. This flat, careful style provides a perfect balance for the intense and tragic content of the novel.

Now turn to the following extract from the same chapter of *Jane Eyre*. Here Jane tells Mr Rochester of the mystery that had so discomposed her earlier in the evening, of the event that had taken place during the preceding might. **As you write about this passage, bring out every detail which adds to the atmosphere of strangeness and doom and show how the climaxes of tension are achieved**.

> 'All the preface, sir; the tale is yet to come. On waking, a gleam dazzled my eyes: I thought – oh, it is daylight! But I was mistaken: it was only candlelight. Sophie, I supposed, had come in. There was a light on the dressing table, and the door of the closet, where, before going to bed, I had hung my wedding-dress and veil, stood open: I heard a rustling there. I asked, "Sophie, what are you doing?" No one answered; but a form emerged from the closet: it took the light, held it aloft, and surveyed the
> 10 garments pendent from the portmanteau. "Sophie! Sophie!" I again cried: and still it was silent. I had risen up in bed; I bent forward: first, surprise, then bewilder-

ment, came over me; and then my blood crept cold through my veins. Mr. Rochester, this was not Sophie, it was not Leah, it was not Mrs. Fairfax: it was not – no, I was sure of it, and am still – it was not even that strange woman, Grace Poole.'

'It must have been one of them,' interrupted my master.

20 'No, sir, I solemnly assure you to the contrary. The shape standing before me had never crossed my eyes within the precincts of Thornfield Hall before; the height, the contour, were new to me.'

'Describe it, Jane.'

'It seemed, sir, a woman, tall and large, with thick and dark hair hanging long down her back. I know not what dress she had on: it was white and straight; but whether gown, sheet, or shroud, I cannot tell.'

'Did you see her face?'

30 'Not at first. But presently she took my veil from its place; she held it up, gazed at it long, and then she threw it over her own head, and turned to the mirror. At that moment I saw the reflection of the visage and features quite distinctly in the dark oblong glass.'

'And how were they?'

'Fearful and ghastly to me – oh, sir, I never saw a face like it! It was a discoloured face – it was a savage face. I wish I could forget the roll of the red eyes and the fearful blackened inflation of the lineaments.'

40 'Ghosts are usually pale, Jane.'

'This, sir, was purple: the lips were swelled and dark; the brow furrowed; the black eyebrows widely raised over the bloodshot eyes. Shall I tell you of what it reminded me?'

'You may.'

'Of the foul German spectre – the Vampyre.'

'Ah? – What did it do?'

'Sir, it removed my veil from its gaunt head, rent it

in two parts, and flinging both on the floor, trampled on
them.'

'Afterwards?'

'It drew aside the window-curtain and looked out:
perhaps it saw dawn approaching, for, taking the candle,
it retreated to the door. Just at my bedside the figure
stopped: the fiery eye glared upon me – she thrust up her
candle close to my face, and extinguished it under my
eyes. I was aware her lurid visage flamed over mine, and
I lost consciousness: for the second time in my life – only
the second time – I became insensible from terror.'

'Who was with you when you revived?'

'No one, sir; but the broad day. I rose, bathed my
head and face in water, drank a long draught; felt that
though enfeebled I was not ill, and determined that to
none but you would I impart this vision. Now, sir, tell
me who and what that woman was?'

'The creature of an over-stimulated brain; that is
certain. I must be careful of you, my treasure: nerves like
yours were not made for rough handling.'

'Sir, depend on it, my nerves were not in fault; the
thing was real: the transaction actually took place.'

'And your previous dreams: were they real too? Is
Thornfield Hall a ruin? Am I severed from you by in-
superable obstacles? Am I leaving you without a tear –
without a kiss – without a word?'

'Not yet.'

'Am I about to do it? – Why, the day is already
commenced which is to bind us indissolubly; and when
we are once united, there shall be no recurrence of these
mental terrors: I guarantee that.'

'Mental terrors, sir! I wish I could believe them to be
only such: I wish it more now than ever ; since even you
cannot explain to me the mystery of that awful visitant.'

'And since I cannot do it, Jane, it must have been
unreal.'

'But, sir, when I said so to myself on rising this morning, and when I looked round the room to gather courage and comfort from the cheerful aspect of each familiar object in full daylight, there – on the carpet – I saw what gave the distinct lie to my hypothesis, – the veil, torn from top to bottom, in two halves!'

90

I felt Mr. Rochester start and shudder; he hastily flung his arms round me.

'Thank God!' he exclaimed, 'that if anything malignant did come near you last night, it was only the veil that was harmed. – Oh, to think what might have happened!'

Charlotte Brontë, *Jane Eyre* (1847)

Intensity

Jane Eyre's search for love and passionate attachment to a man is an expression of Charlotte Brontë's struggle to assert that women have the right to feel, to be passionate and to act on such feelings. It is a right that women, reduced to the role of docile recipients of attention, have been denied by a male-dominated society. Charlotte Brontë is a feminist. Yet fate denies Jane Eyre the full and rapturous experience of passion and we have noted the cross-current of unease, issuing perhaps from sexual fear or guilt, that creates the particular tension of Charlotte Brontë's writing. We may perceive a similar conflict in that intense stormy novel, *Wuthering Heights*, written by Charlotte's younger sister Emily.

More, perhaps, than in the case of most novels, extracts give but a partial sense of the whole of *Wuthering Heights*, for the violence and passion of Catherine Earnshaw's relationship with Heathcliff in the first half of the novel is matched by the calmly restorative growth of young love between her daughter and Hareton in the second half. However, it is with the quality and presentation of that passion that we are concerned here.

The background to the following passage may be briefly summarised: Heathcliff is a foundling, probably of gipsy origin, who has been brought into the Earnshaw household and reared there. He loves the Earnshaws' daughter, Catherine, but Catherine decides to marry Edgar Linton, wealthy heir to a neighbouring estate. In this extract, she talks of her love to the narrator of this part of the novel, the servant Nelly Dean. **Write an appreciation of the passage, bringing out the force of Catherine's feelings and how they are expressed and the importance of the presence of Nelly and of Heathcliff.** Some further questions and comments on the extract follow it but I suggest you write first and then extend your perceptions further by considering the questions.

'If I were in heaven, Nelly, I should be extremely miserable.'

'Because you are not fit to go there,' I answered. 'All sinners would be miserable in heaven.'

'But it is not for that. I dreamt once that I was there.'

'I tell you I won't hearken to your dreams, Miss Catherine! I'll go to bed,' I interrupted again.

She laughted, and held me down; for I made a motion to leave my chair.

10 'This is nothing,' cried she: 'I was only going to say that heaven did not seem to be my home; and I broke my heart with weeping to come back to earth; and the angels were so angry that they flung me out into the middle of the heath on the top of Wuthering Heights; where I woke sobbing for joy. That will do to explain my secret, as well as the other. I've no more business to marry Edgar Linton than I have to be in heaven; and if the wicked man in there had not brought Heathcliff so low, I shouldn't have thought of it. It would degrade me

20 to marry Heathcliff now; so he shall never know how I love him: and that, not because he's handsome, Nelly,

but because he's more myself than I am. Whatever our souls are made of, his and mine are the same; and Linton's is as different as a moonbeam from lightning, or frost from fire.'

Ere this speech ended I became sensible of Heathcliff's presence. Having noticed a slight movement, I turned my head, and saw him rise from the bench, and steal out noiselessly. He had listened till he heard Catherine say it would degrade her to marry him, and then he stayed to hear no further. My companion, sitting on the ground, was prevented by the back of the settle from remarking his presence or departure; but I started, and bade her hush!

'Why?' she asked, gazing nervously round.

'Joseph is here,' I answered catching opportunely the roll of his cartwheels up the road; 'and Heathcliff will come in with him. I'm not sure whether he were not at the door this moment.'

'Oh, he couldn't overhear me at the door!' said she. 'Give me Hareton, while you get the supper, and when it is ready ask me to sup with you. I want to cheat my uncomfortable conscience, and be convinced that Heathcliff has no notion of these things. He has not, has he? He does not know what being in love is!'

'I see no reason that he should not know, as well as you,' I returned; 'and if *you* are his choice, he'll be the most unfortunate creature that ever was born! As soon as you become Mrs. Linton, he loses friend, and love, and all! Have you considered how you'll bear the separation, and how he'll bear to be quite deserted in the world? Because, Miss Catherine—'

'He quite deserted! we separated!' she exclaimed, with an accent of indignation. 'Who is to separate us, pray? They'll meet the fate of Milo! Not as long as I live, Ellen: for no mortal creature. Every Linton on the face of the earth might melt into nothing before I could consent to forsake Heathcliff. Oh, that's not what I intend – that's

not what I mean! I shouldn't be Mrs. Linton were such
a price demanded! He'll be as much to me as he has been
60   all his lifetime. Edgar must shake off his antipathy, and
tolerate him, at least. He will, when he learns my true
feelings towards him. Nelly, I see now you think me a
selfish wretch; but did it never strike you that if Heathcliff and I married, we should be beggars? whereas, if I
marry Linton I can aid Heathcliff to rise, and place him
out of my brother's power.'

'With your husband's money, Miss Catherine?' I
asked. 'You'll find him not so pliable as you calculate
upon: and, though I'm hardly a judge, I think that's the
70   worst motive you've given yet for being the wife of young
Linton.'

'It is not,' retorted she; 'it is the best! The others were
the satisfaction of my whims: and for Edgar's sake, too,
to satisfy him. This is for the sake of one who compre-
hends in his person my feelings to Edgar and myself. I
cannot express it; but surely you and everybody have a
notion that there is or should be an existence of yours
beyond you. What were the use of my creation, if I were
entirely contained here? My great miseries in this world
80   have been Heathcliff's miseries, and I watched and felt
each from the beginning: my great thought in living is
himself. If all else perished, and *he* remained, *I* should
still continue to be; and if all else remained, and he were
annihilated, the universe would turn to a mighty
stranger: I should not seem a part of it. My love for
Linton is like the foliage in the woods: time will change
it, I'm well aware, as winter changes the trees. My love
for Heathcliff resembles the eternal rocks beneath: a
source of little visible delight, but necessary. Nelly, I *am*
90   Heathcliff! He's always, always in my mind: not as a
pleasure, any more than I am always a pleasure to
myself, but as my own being. So don't talk of our
separation again: it is impracticable; and—'

She paused, and hid her face in the folds of my gown; but I jerked it forcibly away. I was out of patience with her folly!

'If I can make any sense of your nonsense, Miss,' I said, 'it only goes to convince me that you are ignorant of the duties you undertake in marrying; or else that you are a wicked, unprincipled girl. But trouble me with no more secrets: I'll not promise to keep them.'

Emily Brontë, *Wuthering Heights* (1847)

1 What relationship does Catherine's dream have to her marital intentions? Do you think she is receptive to the full message of her dream?

2 How does she want to regard Heathcliff and treat him? Is this realistic?

3 What imagery does she use to convey her views of Linton and Heathcliff and of her love for them? You should consider lines 22–25 and 85–89. How appropriate is this imagery?

4 How do the sentiments of Nelly Dean provide a foil for those of Catherine? What sort of narrator is she?

5 Finally, what effect is created and what implications for the rest of the novel arise from the presence, during part of this episode, of Heathcliff? Is it of significance that only Nelly notices him?

Morality

Mary Ann Evans, who wrote under the pseudonym of George Eliot, might also be regarded as a feminist. In *The Mill on the Floss*, she explores the position in mid-Victorian provincial society of a young woman, Maggie Tulliver, whose love of life and vitality is constantly being impeded by the narrow expectations of those around her and by her own internalised religious and moral oppression. Her first love, Philip Wakem, is rejected by her family – their fathers being engaged in interminable legal wranglings – and later she is uneasily aware of being attracted to the charming but unreliable Stephen Guest, who is engaged to her cousin, Lucy. Maggie fights against what rapidly becomes a mutual and mutually acknowledged passion but, at last, it happens that she allows Stephen to lead her into an elopement when, by a series of accidents, they find themselves the only remaining members of a projected boating trip.

Discuss or write about this passage with the following questions and pointers in mind. Some further comments follow it.

1 What is Maggie's state of mind during the first half of the passage and how is it, by implication, assessed in the narrative?
2 Does the elopement seem a sordid, selfish affair?
3 How are circumstances and surroundings used symbolically?
4 Trace the changes in Maggie's feelings as she realises what has happened.
5 How do you feel about Stephen Guest and his words to Maggie?

'Let us go,' Stephen murmured, entreatingly, rising, and taking her hand to raise her too. 'We shall not be long together.'

And they went. Maggie felt that she was being led down the garden among the roses, being helped with firm tender care into the boat, having the cushion and cloak arranged for her feet, and her parasol opened for her (which she had forgotten) – all by this stronger presence that seemed to bear her along without any act of her own
10 will, like the added self which comes with the sudden

exalting influence of a strong tonic – and she felt nothing else. Memory was excluded.

They glided rapidly along, Stephen rowing, helped by the backward-flowing tide, past the Tofton trees and houses – on between the silent sunny fields and pastures, which seemed filled with a natural joy that had no reproach for theirs. The breath of the young, unwearied day, the delicious rhythmic dip of the oars, the fragmentary song of a passing bird heard now and then, as if it were only the overflowing of brimful gladness, the sweet solitude of a twofold consciousness that was mingled into one by that grave untiring gaze which need not be averted – what else could there be in their minds for the first hour? Some low, subdued, languid exclamation of love came from Stephen from time to time, as he went on rowing idly, half automatically: otherwise, they spoke no word; for what could words have been but an inlet to thought? and thought did not belong to that enchanted haze in which they were enveloped – it belonged to the past and the future that lay outside the haze. Maggie was only dimly conscious of the banks, as they passed them, and dwelt with no recognition on the villages: she knew there were several to be passed before they reached Luckreth, where they always stopped and left the boat. At all times she was so liable to fits of absence, that she was likely enough to let her way-marks pass unnoticed.

But at last Stephen, who had been rowing more and more idly, ceased to row, laid down the oars, folded his arms, and looked down on the water as if watching the pace at which the boat glided without his help. This sudden change roused Maggie. She looked at the far-stretching fields – at the banks close by – and felt that they were entirely strange to her. A terrible alarm took possession of her.

'Oh, have we passed Luckreth – where we were to stop?' she exclaimed, looking back to see if the place were

out of sight. No village was to be seen. She turned
round again, with a look of distressed questioning at
Stephen.

50   He went on watching the water, and said, in a strange,
dreamy, absent tone, 'Yes – a long way.'

'Oh, what shall I do?' cried Maggie in an agony. 'We
shall not get home for hours – and Lucy – O God, help
me!'

She clasped her hands and broke into a sob, like a
frightened child: she thought of nothing but of meeting
Lucy, and seeing her look of pained surprise and doubt
– perhaps of just upbraiding.

Stephen moved and sat beside her, and gently drew
60   down the clasped hands.

'Maggie,' he said in a deep tone of slow decision, 'let
us never go home again – till no one can part us – till
we are married.'

The unusual tone, the startling words, arrested
Maggie's sob, and she sat quite still – wondering: as if
Stephen might have seen some possibilities that would
alter everything, and annul the wretched facts.

'See, Maggie, how everything has come without our
seeking – in spite of all our efforts. We never thought of
70   being alone together again: it has all been done by
others. See how the tide is carrying us out – away from
all those unnatural bonds that we have been trying to
make faster round us – and trying in vain. It will carry
us on to Torby, and we can land there, and get some
carriage, and hurry on to York, and then to Scotland –
and never pause a moment till we are bound to each
other, so that only death can part us. It is the only right
thing, dearest: it is the only way of escaping from this
wretched entanglement. Everything has concurred to
80   point it out to us. We have contrived nothing, we have
thought of nothing ourselves.'

George Eliot, *The Mill on the Floss* (1859)

The strength of this writing lies, I believe, in the combination of two qualities: on the one hand, a wholly clear sense of the moral impropriety of the elopement and a condemnation of it and, on the other hand, a profound sympathy with Maggie and a celebration of the feelings of love that she shares with Stephen. It is an impossible dilemma, a conflict that can never be satisfactorily resolved as the outcome of the novel reveals, but it is most subtly and precisely presented here.

From the first Maggie finds herself responding to Stephen's reassurance and command of the situation. His comment that they would not be long together alone is part of a confident physical movement that brings her to her feet and leads her down the garden path, literally and metaphorically. That phrase (line 5) is the first hint of an authorial assessment of the situation which is built into the texture of the narrative. What appears for a moment to be a bed of roses for Maggie (perhaps it *is* too ingenious to relate this colloquial phrase to the reference to roses in line 5?) is in fact a dream, a giving up of her own sense of responsibility, and it is compared with the false exhilaration of a strong drink (line 11). Maggie is not *completely* herself: her memory, her past, and therefore her capacity to foresee the implications of her action are all excluded. The point is made again when George Eliot tells us that words and thoughts 'did not belong to that enchanted haze in which they were enveloped' (lines 28–29). This is magic, enchantment, an unreality that stops them from seeing clearly and even from thinking and conversing as the fully civilised beings they could be. And how appropriate that the entire elopement should take place in circumstances of drift, in a state somewhere between action and inaction, Stephen merely 'rowing idly, half automatically', and Maggie wholly carried along on the current, the drift of events!

On the other hand, there is in this passage the celebration of a joyous intimacy and appreciation of wholesome, natural, youthful vitality. Pick out the adjectives in lines 13–22. The surroundings reflect back to the couple this joy in existence, a joy that transcends the limiting effects of society's moral restraints. We feel the natural goodness of the scene and sympathise with all that seduces Maggie into perpetuating the dream. Even their physical posture in relation to each other seems to justify and encourage 'the sweet solitude of a twofold consciousness' (lines 20–21): they cannot but gaze at each other. It *is* delightful.

Stephen, however, is a good deal more conscious of what is happening than is Maggie. He is, from the start, involved in a seductive activity and is capable of producing, even at the height of the dream, the occasional 'subdued, languid exclamation of love'. It is he who breaks the enchanted haze by laying down his oars and folding his arms, both very deliberate acts, and it is then that reality crowds in on Maggie. We are told that 'she looked at the far-stretching fields – at the banks close by'. The symbolism is clear: she recognises the context of what is happening, both its immediate and more distant implications, and it is the sense of her betrayal of her trusting and loyal cousin, Lucy, that reduces her to being like a frightened child (line 56), another aspect of her abandonment of adult responsibility. Again Stephen takes an initiative, one so bold as to provide Maggie with the illusion that there was a way of escape from all their problems, and, finally, as he follows up the suggestion that they run away and marry, we see the full extent of his duplicity. Notice how he ascribes to other people and to natural forces a situation that he, himself, has engineered. 'We have contrived nothing, we have thought of nothing ourselves,' he says but he has, in fact, just uttered a detailed, geographically realistic plan for their elopement.

Maggie Tulliver is the victim not only of a constraining, narrow-minded society but of an exploitive, chauvinistic man who has robbed her of freedom and denied her the right to make a moral choice. Yet she revives: her personality is too rich and vibrant to be entirely reduced to the level of a passive victim. That evening, she and Stephen are taken on board a trading vessel where they spend the night on deck. The following morning Maggie wakes in a different frame of mind.

Write a full appreciation of this passage concentrating on Maggie's feelings and the way in which her developing thoughts lead to a richer sense of her own being.

She had fallen asleep before nine, and had been sleeping for six hours before the faintest hint of a midsummer daybreak was discernible. She awoke from that vivid dreaming which makes the margin of our deeper rest: she was in a boat on the wide water with Stephen, and in the gathering darkness something like a star appeared, that grew and grew till they saw it was the Virgin seated in St. Ogg's boat, and it came nearer and nearer, till they saw the Virgin was Lucy and the boat-
10   man was Philip – no, not Philip, but her brother, who rowed past without looking at her; and she rose to stretch out her arms and call to him, and their own boat turned over with the movement, and they began to sink, till with one spasm of dread she seemed to awake, and find she was a child again in the parlour at evening twilight, and Tom was not really angry. From the soothed sense of that false waking she passed to the real waking – to the splash of water against the vessel, and the sound of a footstep on the deck, and the awful starlit
20   sky. There was a moment of utter bewilderment before her mind could get disentangled from the confused web of dreams; but soon the whole terrible truth urged itself upon her. Stephen was not by her now: she was alone with her own memory and her own dread. The irrevocable wrong that must blot her life had been committed: she had brought sorrow into the lives of others – into the lives that were knit up with hers by trust and love. The feeling of a few short weeks had hurried her into the sins her nature had most recoiled from – breach of faith and

30   cruel selfishness; she had rent the ties that had given meaning to duty, and made herself an outlawed soul, with no guide but the wayward choice of her own passion. And where would that lead her? – where had it led her now? She had said she would rather die than fall into that temptation. She felt it now – now that the consequences of such a fall had come before the outward act was completed. There was at least this fruit from all her years of striving after the highest and best – that her soul, though betrayed, beguiled, ensnared, could never

40   deliberately consent to a choice of the lower. And a choice of what? O God – not a choice of joy, but of conscious cruelty and hardness; for could she ever cease to see before her Lucy and Philip, with their murdered trust and hopes? Her life with Stephen could have no sacredness: she must for ever sink and wander vaguely, driven by uncertain impulse; for she had let go the clue of life – that clue which once in the far-off years her young need had clutched so strongly. She had renounced all delights then, before she knew them, before they had

50   come within her reach. Philip had been right when he told her that she knew nothing of renunciation: she had thought it was quiet ecstasy; she saw it face to face now – that sad patient living strength which holds the clue of life – and saw that the thorns were for ever pressing on its brow. The yesterday, which could never be revoked – if she could change it now for any length of inward silent endurance, she would have bowed beneath that cross with a sense of rest.

    Daybreak came and the reddening eastern light, while

60   her past life was grasping her in this way, with that tightening clutch which comes in the last moments of possible rescue. She could see Stephen now lying on the deck still fast asleep, and with the sight of him there came a wave of anguish that found its way in a long-suppressed sob. The worst bitterness of parting – the thought that urged

the sharpest inward cry for help, was the pain it must give to *him*. But surmounting everything was the horror of her own possible failure, the dread lest her conscience should be benumbed again, and not rise to energy till it
70 was too late. – Too late! It was too late already not to have caused misery: too late for everything, perhaps, but to rush away from the last act of baseness – the tasting of joys that were wrung from crushed hearts.

The sun was rising now, and Maggie started up with the sense that a day of resistance was beginning for her. Her eye-lashes were still wet with tears, as, with her shawl over her head, she sat looking at the slowly-rounding sun. Something roused Stephen too, and, getting up from his hard bed, he came to sit beside her.
80 The sharp instinct of anxious love saw something to give him alarm in the first glance. He had a hovering dread of some resistance in Maggie's nature that he would be unable to overcome. He had the uneasy consciousness that he had robbed her of perfect freedom yesterday: there was too much native honour in him, for him not to feel that if her will should recoil, his conduct would have been odious, and she would have a right to reproach him.

But Maggie did not feel that right: she was too
90 conscious of fatal weakness in herself – too full of the tenderness that comes with the foreseen need for inflicting a wound. She let him take her hand when he came to sit down beside her, and smiled at him – only with rather a sad glance; she could say nothing to pain him till the moment of possible parting was nearer.

George Eliot, *The Mill on the Floss* (1859)

5 Narrative

There are many ways of telling a story and giving life to fictional characters, of creating the world of a novel. If you have worked through this book, you will now appreciate the range and variety that is possible: from the irony of Jane Austen to the intensity of Sylvia Plath, from the social and political awareness of Aldous Huxley to the personal inwardness of D H Lawrence, from the gothic extremes of the Brontës to the bleak grey vision of George Orwell. In this chapter, we look more closely at some techniques, at methods of constructing a novel and presenting characters. We are here concerned with style rather than content, though as we proceed you will appreciate how false it is to attempt to separate the one from the other.

Double vision

Dickens's great novel *Bleak House* is composed of two narratives which interleave with each other: part of the tale is unfolded by someone who apparently knows all there is to know about each character and who perceives the ironies and results of every action, who sees consequences that lie far beyond the knowledge of any one character; the other part of the tale is told, as a sort of reminiscence or journal, by Esther Summerson, a character who is contained within the complex plot. Esther narrates all those episodes in which she appears and her style is quite different from that of the omniscient narrator.

Let us consider short representative extracts from these two narratives. The background to the first is soon told: Jo is a street urchin, a crossing-sweeper, one of the most impoverished members of society. The background to the second extract is more complex: Esther is illegitimate, believed by her mother to have died at birth but, in fact, brought up secretly by a narrow-minded, unloving, puritanical aunt who has drummed into Esther a sense of the sinfulness of her origin. In the passage quoted below, she refers to herself as being 'changed', the result of a serious, contagious disease that has destroyed her good looks. **Compare and contrast the impact upon you of these two extracts from the same novel and pick out all the points of difference you can find**. A detailed commentary follows the extracts.

Jo comes out of Tom-all-Alone's, meeting the tardy morning which is always late in getting down there, and munches his dirty bit of bread as he comes along. His way lying through many streets, and the houses not yet being open, he sits down to breakfast on the door-step of the Society for the Propagation of the Gospel in Foreign Parts, and gives it a brush when he has finished, as an acknowledgment of the accommodation. He admires the size of the edifice, and wonders what it's all
10 about. He has no idea, poor wretch, of the spiritual destitution of a coral reef in the Pacific, or what it costs to look up the precious souls among the cocoa-nuts and bread-fruit.

He goes to his crossing, and begins to lay it out for the day. The town awakes; the great tee-totum* is set up for its daily spin and whirl; all that unaccountable reading and writing, which has been suspended for a few hours, recommences. Jo, and the other lower animals, get on in the unintelligible mess as they can. It is market-day. The
20 blinded oxen, over-goaded, over-driven, never guided, run into wrong places and are beaten out; and plunge, red-eyed and foaming, at stone walls; and often sorely

* *tee-totum*: kind of spinning top marked with letters, used for playing a game of chance.

hurt the innocent, and often sorely hurt themselves. Very like Jo and his order; very, very like!

I looked at her; but I could not see her, I could not hear her, I could not draw my breath. The beating of my heart was so violent and wild, that I felt as if my life were breaking from me. But when she caught me to her breast, kissed me, wept over me, compassionated me, and called me back to myself; when she fell on her knees and cried to me, 'O my child, my child, I am your wicked and unhappy mother! O try to forgive me!' – when I saw her at my feet on the bare earth in her great agony of mind, I felt, through all my tumult of emotion, a burst of gratitude to the providence of God that I was so changed as that I never could disgrace her by any trace of likeness; as that nobody could ever now look at me, and look at her, and remotely think of any near tie between us.

Charles Dickens, *Bleak House* (1853)

Tom-all-Alone's is a slum where Jo lives and, as he makes his way in the early morning to the street crossing where he sweeps and begs, the narrator emphasises the deprivations of his life. Even the sun is reluctant actually to shine in the slums and all Jo has to eat is a dirty bit of bread. There is heavy irony in Jo's sitting down to eat his breakfast on the steps of a charitable missionary institution, which performs an irrelevant function in foreign parts, when he should himself be the recipient of charity in England. The narrator takes up the issue with pointed anger and conveys the misguided arrogance of those who, concerning themselves with 'the spiritual destitution of a coral reef in the Pacific', see Jo as a 'poor wretch', not because he *is* poor but because he is unaware.

So the omniscient narrator unfolds his tale in the context of a trenchant criticism of society, a criticism that is even more forcefully made in the second paragraph of this short passage.

The life of London is likened to a mere toy, one which confuses letters and results in chance winnings for participants in the game. The narrator derides the bureaucratic nonsense of modern life – 'all that unaccountable reading and writing' – and its dangerous class structure which excludes the 'lower animals' from awareness of what is happening. The comparison between the wretched oxen, reduced to a level of bestial frustration and dangerous wildness, and the class of which Jo is representative is drawn out very clearly and forcefully. Such frustration, it is implied, may be the seed of revolution. This narrator sees all that is happening and reveals it to us; his knowledge is complete and his tone is confident. At times his manner is more that of an angry writer of a tract or sermon than what we might expect of a story-teller. Finally, we should observe that he writes in the present tense.

Esther, however, is immersed in the material she writes about. Her vision is partial, limited in space and time to the actual experiences to which she has been exposed. This single paragraph describes one of the most moving and traumatic moments in her life, when the grand socialite, Lady Dedlock, near whose country mansion she is convalescing after illness, reveals herself to Esther as her mother, and yet most of Esther's statements suggest limitation of her perceptions: 'I could not see her, I could not hear her. . . . I felt as if life were breaking from me' (lines 25–28). Esther's partial vision contrasts with the omniscience of the objective narrator but she too knows more than we do and must retain some pieces of information until later in the story. So, she unfolds a personal history, appropriately in the past tense.

Here Esther enables us to experience passionate personal feeling, the dramatic immediacy of her mother falling on her knees and the extremity of her own reaction. One senses behind this intense physical enactment – Lady Dedlock catching Esther to her breast, kissing her, weeping over her, sorrowing for her and then, almost histrionically, falling on her knees – Dickens's own vital interest in the theatre and enjoyment of amateur dramatics. But what did you make of the sentiment that these events prompt in Esther's heart and mind? She thanks God that she is now so disfigured, her looks so destroyed by her illness that others will not recognise that she is Lady Dedlock's daughter. The implications are as fearful and as much an indictment of Victorian moral understanding as the narrator's more pointed statements in the first extract, for Esther constitutes a remarkably powerful portrait of the illegitimate child in a moralistic society. She seems here to see herself as the personification of sin and shame and as a terrible liability to her mother and her self-denigration extends to her regarding personal disfigurement as a blessing. There are many occasions in our reading of Esther's narrative when we squirm with unease at the extent to which she denies herself personal validity.

Here now for your appreciation are two more substantial extracts from *Bleak House*. Each is followed by some questions which you may use to guide your thinking as you discuss or write about the passages.

In his chambers, Mr Tulkinghorn sits meditating an application to the nearest magistrate to-morrow morning for a warrant. Gridley, a disappointed suitor, has been here to-day, and has been alarming. We are not to be put in bodily fear, and that ill-conditioned fellow shall be held to bail again. From the ceiling, foreshortened Allegory, in the person of one impossible Roman upside down, points with the arm of Samson (out of joint, and an odd one) obtrusively toward the window. Why should 10 Mr Tulkinghorn, for such no-reason, look out of window? Is the hand not always pointing there? So he does not look out of window.

And if he did, what would it be to see a woman going by? There are women enough in the world, Mr Tulkinghorn thinks — too many; they are at the bottom of all that goes wrong in it, though, for the matter of that, they create business for lawyers. What would it be to see a woman going by, even though she were going secretly? They are all secret. Mr Tulkinghorn knows that, very well.

But they are not all like the woman who now leaves him and his house behind; between whose plain dress, and her refined manner, there is something exceedingly inconsistent. She should be an upper servant by her attire, yet, in her air and step, though both are hurried and assumed — as far as she can assume in the muddy streets, which she treads with an unaccustomed foot — she is a lady. Her face is veiled, and still she sufficiently betrays herself to make more than one of those who pass her look round sharply.

She never turns her head. Lady or servant, she has a purpose in her, and can follow it. She never turns her head, until she comes to the crossing where Jo plies with his broom. He crosses with her, and begs. Still, she does not turn her head until she has landed on the other side. Then, she slightly beckons to him, and says, 'Come here!'

The woman questions Jo about an obscure man who has recently died and asks to be shown the places in which he lived and worked and, finally, his grave. . .

'He was put there,' says Jo, holding to the bars and looking in.

'Where? O, what a scene of horror!'

'There!' says Jo, pointing. 'Over yinder. Among them piles of bones, and close to that there kitchin winder! They put him wery nigh the top. They was obliged to stamp upon it to git it in. I could unkiver it for you with my broom, if the gate was open. That's why they locks it, I s'pose,' giving it a shake. 'It's always locked. Look at the rat!' cries Jo, excited. 'Hi! Look! There he goes! Ho! Into the ground!'

The servant shrinks into a corner – into a corner of
that hideous archway, with its deadly stains contami-
nating her dress; and putting out her two hands, and
passionately telling him to keep away from her, for he
is loathsome to her, so remains for some moments. Jo
stands staring, and is still staring when she recovers herself.

'Is this place of abomination, consecrated ground?'

'I don't know nothink of consequential ground,' says
Jo, still staring.

'Is it blessed?'

'WHICH?' says Jo, in the last degree amazed.

'Is it blessed?'

'I'm blest if I know,' says Jo, staring more than ever;
'but I shouldn't think it warn't. Blest?' repeats Jo, something troubled in his mind. 'It an't done it much good
if it is. Blest? I should think it was t'othered myself. But
I don't know nothink!'

The servant takes as little heed of what he says, as she
seems to take of what she has said herself. She draws off
her glove, to get some money from her purse. Jo silently
notices how white and small her hand is, and what a jolly
servant she must be to wear such sparkling rings.

She drops a piece of money in his hand, without
touching it, and shuddering as their hands approach.
'Now,' she adds, 'show me the spot again!'

Jo thrusts the handle of his broom between the bars
of the gate, and with his utmost power of elaboration,
points it out. At length, looking aside to see if he has
made himself intelligible, he finds that he is alone.

Charles Dickens, *Bleak House* (1853)

1 Who do you suppose Mr Tulkinghorn to be and what
might be his role in the novel?

2 How are we made particularly aware of the all-seeing eye
of the narrator in the first few paragraphs?

3 How many questions are there in the first two paragraphs? What is the effect of asking questions? Try to define the tone of the narrative.

4 How many areas of uncertainty or mystery can you find here?

5 Find all the moments which emphasise that Jo and the lady come from opposite ends of the social spectrum. How does this fact contribute to the drama of the encounter?

6 Discuss the effects created by the gestures and movements of the characters.

7 Finally, what feelings and speculations does the passage arouse?

We turn now to a passage from Esther's narrative. She and her close friend, Ada, have been taken by a philanthropic busybody, Mrs Pardiggle, to visit a desperately poor family. The men, in particular, intensely resent their presence.

We were much relieved, under these circumstances, when Mrs Pardiggle left off. The man on the floor then turning his head round again, said morosely,

'Well! You've done, have you?

'For today, I have, my friend. But I am never fatigued. I shall come to you again, in your regular order,' returned Mrs Pardiggle with demonstrative cheerfulness.

'So long as you goes now,' said he, folding his arms and shutting his eyes with an oath, 'you may do wot you
10   like!'

Mrs Pardiggle accordingly rose, and made a little vortex in the confined room from which the pipe itself very narrowly escaped. Taking one of her young family in each hand, and telling the others to follow closely, and expressing her hope that the brickmaker and all his house would be improved when she saw them next, she then proceeded to another cottage. I hope it is not unkind of me to say that she certainly did make, in this,

20 as in everything else, a show that was not conciliatory, of doing charity by wholesale, and of dealing in it to a large extent.

She supposed that we were following her; but as soon as the space was left clear, we approached the woman sitting by the fire, to ask if the baby were ill.

She only looked at it as it lay on her lap. We had observed before that when she looked at it she covered her discoloured eye with her hand, as though she wished to separate any association with noise and violence and ill-treatment, from the poor little child.

30 Ada, whose gentle heart was moved by its appearance, bend down to touch its little face. As she did so, I saw what happened and drew her back. The child died.

'O Esther!' cried Ada, sinking on her knees beside it. 'Look here! O Esther, my love, the little thing! The suffering, quiet, pretty little thing! I am so sorry for it. I am so sorry for the mother. I never saw a sight so pitiful as this before! O baby, baby!'

Such compassion, such gentleness, as that with which she bent down weeping, and put her hand upon the

40 mother's, might have softened any mother's heart that ever beat. The woman at first gazed at her in astonishment, and then burst into tears.

Presently I took the light burden from her lap; did what I could to make the baby's rest the prettier and gentler; laid it on a shelf, and covered it with my own handkerchief. We tried to comfort the mother, and we whispered to her what Our Saviour said of children. She answered nothing, but sat weeping – weeping very much.

When I turned, I found that the young man had taken

50 out the dog, and was standing at the door looking in upon us; with dry eyes, but quiet. The girl was quiet too, and sat in a corner looking on the ground. The man had risen. He still smoked his pipe with an air of defiance, but he was silent.

An ugly woman, very poorly clothed, hurried in while
I was glancing at them, and coming straight up to the
mother, said, 'Jenny! Jenny!' The mother rose on being
so addressed, and fell upon the woman's neck.

60 She also had upon her face and arms the marks of ill-
usage. She had no kind of grace about her, but the grace
of sympathy, but when she condoled with the woman,
and her own tears fell she wanted no beauty. I say
condoled, but her only words were 'Jenny! Jenny!' All the
rest was in the tone in which she said them.

I thought it very touching to see these two women,
coarse and shabby and beaten, so united; to see what
they could be to one another; to see how they felt for one
another; how the heart of each to each was softened by
the hard trials of their lives. I think the best side of such
70 people is almost hidden from us. What the poor are to
the poor is little known, excepting to themselves and
GOD.

Charles Dickens, *Bleak House* (1853)

1 Everything is sifted through Esther's ways of seeing and
thinking. Which details in the passage help you to understand her character? Does she judge or evaluate what
happens around her?
2 Consider Ada's response to the death of the baby and how
Esther, in turn, responds to Ada's outburst.
3 Find all the details which help to develop the pathos, the
sadness of this scene.

Implied judgement

Both the narrators of *Bleak House* judge the society of their day
and convey an alertly critical attitude towards characters and
circumstances: the omniscient narrator is angry, openly

condemning; Esther, in her humbler way, dares to criticise or more often to emphatically celebrate the goodness she can find around her. A less overt or obvious way of assessing whilst describing may be found in *Dubliners* by James Joyce. This book is a collection of short stories, not a novel, but so coherent and insistent is Joyce's view of Dublin life that the collection of separate pieces feels very much a single work, informed throughout with a single vision. Take the opening of this story. What impression is created of Little Chandler? Joyce is a very economical writer and every detail should be considered.

Eight years before he had seen his friend off at the North Wall and wished him godspeed. Gallaher had got on. You could tell that at once by his travelled air, his well-cut tweed suit, and fearless accent. Few fellows had talents like his and fewer still could remain unspoiled by such success. Gallaher's heart was in the right place and he had deserved to win. It was something to have a friend like that.

10   Little Chandler's thoughts ever since lunch-time had been of his meeting with Gallaher, of Gallaher's invitation and of the great city London where Gallaher lived. He was called Little Chandler because, though he was but slightly under the average stature, he gave one the idea of being a little man. His hands were white and small, his frame was fragile, his voice was quiet and his manners were refined. He took the greatest care of his fair silken hair and moustache and used perfume discreetly on his handkerchief. The half-moons of his nails were perfect and when he smiled you caught a

20   glimpse of a row of childish white teeth.

As he sat at his desk in the King's Inns he thought what changes those eight years had brought. The friend whom he had known under a shabby and necessitous guise had become a brilliant figure on the London Press.

He turned often from his tiresome writing to gaze out of the office window. The glow of a late autumn sunset covered the grass plots and walks. It cast a shower of kindly golden dust on the untidy nurses and decrepit old men who drowsed on the benches; it flickered upon all the moving figures – on the children who ran screaming along the gravel paths and on everyone who passed through the gardens. He watched the scene and thought of life; and (as always happened when he thought of life) he became sad. A gentle melancholy took possession of him. He felt how useless it was to struggle against fortune, this being the burden of wisdom which the ages had bequeathed to him.

He remembered the books of poetry upon his shelves at home. He had bought them in his bachelor days and many an evening, as he sat in the little room off the hall, he had been tempted to take one down from the bookshelf and read out something to his wife. But shyness had always held him back; and so the books had remained on their shelves. At times he repeated lines to himself and this consoled him.

When his hour had struck he stood up and took leave of his desk and of his fellow-clerks punctiliously. He emerged from under the feudal arch of the King's Inns, a neat modest figure, and walked swiftly down Henrietta Street. The golden sunset was waning and the air had grown sharp. A horde of grimy children populated the street. They stood or ran in the roadway or crawled up the steps before the gaping doors or squatted like mice upon the thresholds. Little Chandler gave them no thought. He picked his way deftly through all that minute vermin-like life and under the shadow of the gaunt spectral mansions in which the old nobility of Dublin had roistered. No memory of the past touched him, for his mind was full of a present joy.

James Joyce, 'A Little Cloud', *Dubliners* (1914)

The passage begins by inviting us to consider the quality of Little Chandler's thoughts. It is a type of reported monologue: Joyce describes to us the stream of thoughts that flows through his character's mind and, as the story develops, we move in and out of his mind, either observing him externally, in action, or internally, hearing what he is thinking. What do we learn about him from that first paragraph? He is idolising a friend, someone who has left Dublin and, we later learn, has a job writing for a London newspaper. Little Chandler thinks of Gallaher in well-worn phrases of clichéd admiration: humdrum expressions like 'seen . . . off', 'wished him godspeed', 'got on','unspoiled by success', 'heart in the right place', 'deserved to win', suggest a mediocre mind that deals in only second-hand language. He seems also to be easily impressed by the most superficial of changes – 'his travelled air, his well-cut tweed suit, and fearless accent' (lines 3–4) – and to be willing to admire his friend at the expense of his own self-respect.

We sense that there is something naïve and immature about Little Chandler, so obsessed is he with the invitation to meet Gallaher for a drink. Joyce's description of his appearance bears out this initial impression. Although he is of almost normal height, he seems small, lacking in substance, pre-occupied with sterile personal tidiness and good manners. His pernickety dress suggests a defensive self-preoccupation that has kept him 'childish'.

Little Chandler's job is apparently that of a legal copyist. He works in the King's Inns, the offices of Dublin lawyers, and there is a reference to the 'tiresome writing' that he is engaged in.

He is clearly bored and dissatisfied with his own work and contrasts himself with Gallaher, now 'a brilliant figure on the London press'. Why has Little Chandler not 'got on'? The reasons are made clear in his characteristic way of thinking, observing and being detached from real life.

We see him observing the scene outside: he sees the 'late autumn sunset' making the representatives of suffering humanity, 'untidy nurses and decrepit old men', glow 'in a shower of golden dust'. It is a conveniently romantic response, a way of escaping confrontation with reality by casting a veil of gentle, illusory, transient beauty over the people. He retreats into an indulgent, passive melancholy. Nor is he refreshed by his cultural tradition: what he has received from it is a 'burden of wisdom', something to be borne. Again the language is clichéd, dead; what has been 'bequeathed' to him is stoical endurance, not vitality or stimulation. He is at one with the dead past.

This lack of contact with real vibrant life is elaborated in the last two paragraphs of the extract. Little Chandler has cut himself off from the restorative effects of poetry, his marriage having inhibited him and turned him into something of a frustrated artist or aesthete. His experience of poetry, which once had some power over him, is now reduced to repeating familiar lines to himself: he is never exposed to anything new or demanding.

Similarly, when he leaves his office, the romantic glow of the early evening is waning into cold reality and he too is now exposed to the teeming life of the Dublin streets. The children are described as 'a horde', squatting 'like mice', as 'minute vermin-like life': the comparisons suggest his complete failure to respond with warmth or humanity. He is cut off from his surroundings and from the past which might give him insight, passively imprisoned in his version of unreality. And his surroundings seem to echo his condition (or perhaps his condition, similar to that of many characters in *Dubliners*, is but a product of his surroundings) for we are told that the slums through which Little Chandler passes were once the 'mansions in which the old nobility had roistered'.

It is clear that an implied judgement is present in almost every sentence of this story, though the issue is whether we sympathise with or condemn Little Chandler.

Here, for your own analysis, is a passage from towards the end of the story. In the meantime, Little Chandler has met

Gailaher, whom we perceive to be an utterly worthless, vulgar and mercenary person, and has then returned home. His wife slips out to buy something before the shops close and leaves him looking after the baby. **As you write about the passage, try to allow each detail to contribute towards your understanding of Little Chandler.**

A little lamp with a white china shade stood upon the table and its light fell over a photograph which was enclosed in a frame of crumpled horn. It was Annie's photograph. Little Chandler looked at it, pausing at the thin tight lips. She wore the pale blue summer blouse which he had brought her home as a present one Saturday. It had cost him ten and elevenpence; but what an agony of nervousness it had cost him! How he had suffered that day, waiting at the shop door until the shop
10   was empty, standing at the counter and trying to appear at his ease while the girl piled ladies' blouses before him, paying at the desk and forgetting to take up the odd penny of his change, being called back by the cashier, and, finally, striving to hide his blushes as he left the shop by examining the parcel to see if it was securely tied. When he brought the blouse home Annie kissed him and said it was very pretty and stylish; but when she heard the price she threw the blouse on the table and said it was a regular swindle to charge ten and eleven-
20   pence for that. At first she wanted to take it back but when she tried it on she was delighted with it, especially with the make of the sleeves, and kissed him and said he was very good to think of her.

Hm!. . .

He looked coldly into the eyes of the photograph and they answered coldly. Certainly they were pretty and the face itself was pretty. But he found something mean in it. Why was it so unconscious and lady-like? The

composure of the eyes irritated him. They repelled him
and defied him: there was no passion in them, no
rapture. He thought of what Gallaher had said about
rich Jewesses. Those dark Oriental eyes, he thought, how
full they are of passion, of voluptuous longing!. . . Why
had he married the eyes in the photograph?

He caught himself up at the question and glanced
nervously round the room. He found something mean in
the pretty furniture which he had bought for his house
on the hire system. Annie had chosen it herself and it
reminded him of her. It too was prim and pretty. A dull
resentment against his life awoke within him. Could he
not escape from his little house? Was it too late for him
to try to live bravely like Gallaher? Could he go to
London? There was the furniture still to be paid for. If
he could only write a book and get it published, that
might open the way for him.

A volume of Byron's poems lay before him on the
table. He opened it cautiously with his left hand lest he
should waken the child and began to read the first poem
in the book:

Hushed are the winds and still the evening gloom,
Not e'en a Zephyr wanders through the grove,
Whilst I return to view my Margaret's tomb
And scatter flowers on the dust I love.

He paused. He felt the rhythm of the verse about him
in the room. How melancholy it was! Could he, too, write
like that, express the melancholy of his soul in verse?
There were so many things he wanted to describe: his
sensation of a few hours before on Grattan Bridge, for
example. If he could get back again into that mood. . . .

The child awoke and began to cry. He turned from the
page and tried to hush it: but it would not be hushed.
He began to rock it to and fro in his arms but its wailing

111

cry grew keener. He rocked it faster while his eyes began to read the second stanza:

> *Within this narrow cell reclines her clay,*
> *That clay where once . . .*

It was useless. He couldn't read. He couldn't do anything. The wailing of the child pierced the drum of his ear. It was useless, useless! He was a prisoner for life. His arms trembled with anger and suddenly bending to the child's face he shouted:
— Stop!

James Joyce, 'A Little Cloud', *Dubliners* (1914)

Narrator and hero

The narrative method used by Joseph Conrad in a number of his novels is in some respects similar to those of *Bleak House* and *Dubliners*. *Lord Jim* is a particularly good example. This novel is about a man who wanted to be a hero and who is in many ways cast in an heroic mould but who at crucial moments fails. Early in his career he has, as one of the officers of a crippled ship, been induced to abandon it and its three hundred passengers in a moment of high crisis. He is a romantic, a dreamer, sees himself as the man of action but, in the final analysis, is not capable of significant and consistent action. Jim's life, the life of an outsider, is conveyed to us largely through the yarning, the narrative of Captain Marlow, who is swiftly established as a reasonable, reliable guide, a man of the world, captain of his own ship, a sound judge of character. Moreover, he is a conventional figure, a member of the establishment, and so contrasts with Jim, the flawed individualist, the man of intense aspiration and of incapacity ultimately to realise that aspiration. In *Lord Jim* a continuous process of assessment of the hero is carried on both through the narrator and through descriptive elements that contain a wealth of symbolic significance.

Consider the following passage which occurs just after Jim, through the efforts of Marlow, has been offered a fresh start, a chance to put behind him all taint of former failure. As you analyse the passage, try to evaluate both Jim's manner and Marlow's perception of him. Notice their differing styles of utterance. Is there anything about Jim's physical presence which seems to symbolise his inner condition? The ring referred to is an important token whereby Jim may gain acceptance in the remote place to which he is being sent as a trading clerk. **Write your own analysis before you read the commentary that follows the passage**.

'He impressed, almost frightened, me with his elated rattle. He was voluble like a youngster on the eve of a long holiday with a prospect of delightful scrapes, and such an attitude of mind in a grown man and in this connexion had in it something phenomenal, a little mad, dangerous, unsafe. I was on the point of entreating him to take things seriously when he dropped his knife and fork (he had begun eating, or rather swallowing food, as it were, unconsciously), and began to search all round
10 his plate. The ring! The ring! Where the devil . . . Ah! Here it was. . . . He closed his big hand on it, and tried all his pockets one after another. Jove! wouldn't do to lose the thing. He meditated gravely over his fist. Had it? Would hang the bally affair round his neck! And he proceeded to do this immediately, producing a string (which looked like a bit of cotton shoe-lace) for the purpose. There! That would do the trick! It would be the deuce if . . . He seemed to catch sight of my face for the first time, and it steadied him a little. I probably didn't
20 realize, he said with a naïve gravity, how much import-ance he attached to that token. It meant a friend; and

it is a good thing to have a friend. He knew something about that. He nodded at me expressively, but before my disclaiming gesture he leaned his head on his hand and for a while sat silent, playing thoughtfully with the bread-crumbs on the cloth. . . . "Slam the door – that was jolly well put," he cried, and jumping up, began to pace the room, reminding me by the set of the shoulders, the turn of his head, the head-long and uneven stride,
30   of that night when he had paced thus, confessing, explaining – what you will – but, in the last instance, living – living before me, under his own little cloud, with all his unconscious subtlety which could draw consolation from the very source of sorrow. It was the same mood, the same and different, like a fickle companion that today guiding you on the true path, with the same eyes, the same step, the same impulse, tomorrow will lead you hopelessly astray. His tread was assured, his straying, darkened eyes seemed to search the room for
40   something. One of his footfalls somehow sounded louder than the other – the fault of his boots probably – and gave a curious impression of an invisible halt in his gait. One of his hands was rammed deep into his trousers-pocket, the other waved suddenly above his head. "Slam the door!" he shouted. "I've been waiting for that, I'll show yet . . . I'll . . . I'm ready for any confounded thing. . . . I've been dreaming of it . . . Jove! Get out of this. Jove! This is luck at last. . . . You wait. I'll . . ."

'He tossed his head fearlessly, and I confess that for
50   the first and last time in our acquaintance I perceived myself unexpectedly to be thoroughly sick of him. Why these vapourings? He was stumping about the room flourishing his arm absurdly, and now and then feeling on his breast for the ring under his clothes. Where was the sense of such exaltation in a man appointed to be a trading-clerk, and in a place where there was no trade – at that? Why hurl defiance at the universe? This was

not a proper frame of mind to approach any undertaking;
an improper frame of mind not only for him, I said, but
60   for any man. He stood still over me. Did I think so? he
asked, by no means subdued, and with a smile in which
I seemed to detect suddenly something insolent. But then
I am twenty years his senior. Youth *is* insolent; it is its
right – its necessity; it has got to assert itself, and all
assertion in this world of doubts is a defiance, is an
insolence. He went off into a far corner, and coming
back, he, figuratively speaking, turned to rend me. I
spoke like that because I – even I, who had been no end
kind to him – even I remembered – remembered –
70   against him – what – what had happened. And what about
others – the – the world? Where's the wonder he wanted
to get out, meant to get out, meant to stay out – by
heavens! And I talked about proper frames of mind!

'"It is not I or the world who remembers," I shouted.
"It is you – you, who remember." '

Joseph Conrad, *Lord Jim* (1900)

Throughout the passage we are aware of two matters: the way
Jim is reacting to the fresh opportunity before him and the way
Marlow is assessing Jim's reaction. It is Marlow's concern for
his immature attitude that first comes to the fore: he sees Jim
as 'a youngster on the eve of a long holiday', seeing the tasks
before him as no more than 'delightful scrapes'. Marlow
roundly criticises Jim's manner as 'dangerous, unsafe' and, as
he watches him, he thinks back to an occasion you will recall
if you have read the novel, the occasion when Jim confessed,
explained his earlier failure. The thought here (lines
28–34) is complex. Even in his desperation, Marlow had
found Jim an attractive figure, 'in the last instance, living –
living before me', the embodiment of vibrancy and a capacity
for regeneration. He appreciates the young man's ability to
struggle inwardly and to hope. Yet it is, he points out, an

ambivalent quality, an enthusiastic hopefulness that may be fine in some circumstances but disastrous in others. And so it is appropriate that Marlow should see Jim as searching, unsatisfied, restless, with his 'straying, darkened eyes', for Jim does not see things clearly. It is also appropriate that he seems to Marlow to be walking in an uneven way, for the impression of 'an invisible halt in his gait' reinforces, even symbolises, our sense of his unbalanced personality. Likewise, one hand is in a defensive posture, 'rammed deep into his trousers-pocket', whilst the other waves over his head expansively. He is a strange mixture of opposites.

A little later his flamboyant exaltation is countered by a fumbling to find the ring, his security, his passport to acceptance. That very security is, however, attached to him by no more than 'a bit of cotton shoe-lace'. Like so many details in the passage, it symbolises Jim's lack of firm foundations, his essential instability.

Marlow cannot contain himself and refers to Jim's assertions of future success as 'vapourings' but Jim's defence (lines 67–73) is to indulge in a sort of self-pity caused by the way he believes that others now see him. They remember his former failure and hold it against him. He cannot see that Marlow's criticism is an objective and just one, a response to the unsound, irritating and dangerous mood that he has been projecting. Jim is also so self-concerned that he does not realise that the world has more important matters to remember than *his* former failure of nerve. It is this fact that Marlow seeks to bring home to him at the end of the passage.

One further point: there is a world of difference between Marlow's subtle, careful utterances, which imply so much more than they state, and the schoolboy slang, the language of the romantic adventure story, that Jim habitually uses. Take, for example, the sentence in which Marlow describes Jim's uneven steps (lines 40–42): how tentative he apparently is; words like 'somehow', 'sounded', 'probably', 'impression' reflect his groping search for understanding of Jim.

Throughout his narrative he is defining and redefining his explanations or observations and here he offers a purely physical explanation '– the fault of his boots probably', which subtly raises a question rather than provides an answer. In contrast, Jim's slang permeates and devalues most of what he says – 'Where the devil', 'the bally affair', 'it would be the deuce', 'jolly well put'. He is still a lad at heart, living out his cherished fictions.

Jim goes to Patusan and in that remote part of the East makes a success of his job as a trading clerk, becomes a champion of justice and right and a loved protector of the people. Marlow visits him there bearing a message from Stein, Jim's employer. **Write a detailed appreciation of the following passage bearing these points in mind**:

1 the associations and ideas suggested by Marlow's description of the moonlight, the river and the houses of Patusan
2 Jim's attitude here, his feelings about the place and people
3 Marlow's reflections on Jim's position in Patusan and observations of him.

'He spoke thus to me before his house on that evening I've mentioned – after we had watched the moon float away above the chasm between the hills like an ascending spirit out of a grave; its sheen descended, cold and pale, like the ghost of dead sunlight. There is something haunting in the light of the moon; it has all the dispassionateness of a disembodied soul, and something of its inconceivable mystery. It is to our sunshine, which – say what you like – is all we have to live by, what the echo is to the sound: misleading and confusing whether the note be mocking or sad. It robs all forms of matter – which, after all, is our domain – of their substance, and gives a sinister reality to shadows alone. And the

117

shadows were very real around us, but Jim by my side looked very stalwart, as though nothing – not even the occult power of moonlight – could rob him of his reality in my eyes. Perhaps, indeed, nothing could touch him since he had survived the assault of the dark powers. All was silent, all was still; even on the river the moonbeams

20 slept as on a pool. It was the moment of high water, a moment of immobility that accentuated the utter isolation of this lost corner of the earth. The houses crowding along the wide shining sweep without ripple or glitter, stepping into the water in a line of jostling, vague, grey, silvery forms mingled with black masses of shadow, were like a spectral herd of shapeless creatures pressing forward to drink in a spectral and lifeless stream. Here and there a red gleam twinkled within the bamboo walls, warm, like a living spark, significant of human affections,

30 of shelter, of repose.

'He confessed to me that he often watched these tiny warm gleams go out one by one, that he loved to see people go to sleep under his eyes, confident in the security of tomorrow. "Peaceful here, eh?" he asked. He was not eloquent, but there was a deep meaning in the words that followed. "Look at these houses; there's not one where I am not trusted. Jove! I told you I would hang on. Ask any man, woman, or child . . ." He paused. "Well, I am all right anyhow."

40 'I observed quickly that he had found that out in the end. I had been sure of it, I added. He shook his head. "Were you?" He pressed my arm lightly above the elbow. "Well, then – you were right."

'There was elation and pride, there was awe almost, in that low exclamation. "Jove!" he cried, "only think what it is to me." Again he pressed my arm. "And you asked me whether I thought of leaving. Good God! I want to leave! Especially now after what you told me of Mr Stein's . . . Leave! Why! That's what I was afraid of.

50　It would have been – it would have been harder than dying. No – on my word. Don't laugh. I must feel – every day, every time I open my eyes – that I am trusted – that nobody has a right – don't you know? Leave! For where? What for? To get what?"

'I had told him (indeed it was the main object of my visit) that it was Stein's intention to present him at once with the house and the stock of trading goods, on certain easy conditions which would make the transaction perfectly regular and valid. He began to snort and plunge
60　at first. "Confound your delicacy!" I shouted. "It isn't Stein at all. It's giving you what you had made for yourself. And in any case keep your remarks for M' Neil* – when you meet him in the other world. I hope it won't happen soon. . . ." He had to give in to my arguments, because all his conquests, the trust, the fame, the friendships, the love – all these things that made him master had made him a captive, too. He looked with an owner's eye at the peace of the evening, at the river, at the houses, at the everlasting life of the forests, at the life of
70　the old mankind, at the secrets of the land, at the pride of his own heart: but it was they that possessed him and made him their own to the innermost thought, to the slightest stir of blood, to his last breath.'

Joseph Conrad, *Lord Jim* (1900)

* M'Neil was Jim's predecessor as Stein's agent in Patusan.

Multiple consciousness

In this chapter we have been concerned with what might be termed 'angles of vision', the position assumed by the narrator who tells a story. That position may be the intimate but limited view of the autobiographical narrator, as in Esther's narrative in *Bleak House*, or the god-like, omniscient stance of the other narrator of that novel. The writer may choose to enter the minds of his characters and see external events from behind their eyes, as Joyce does in *Dubliners*, or the events and persons of a novel might be sifted through the awareness of a spectator like Marlow who takes but a peripheral part in the action. It is a further development, and a particularly modern one, when the author presents experience from within the consciousness of a number of characters.

Read the following passage with care and concentration. It is not easy to follow its long and complex sentences and, as you read it, try to define the different viewpoints from which the material of the passage is projected.

'Yes, of course, if it's fine tomorrow,' said Mrs Ramsay. 'But you'll have to be up with the lark,' she added.

To her son these words conveyed an extraordinary joy, as if it were settled the expedition were bound to take place, and the wonder to which he had looked forward, for years and years it seemed, was, after a night's darkness and a day's sail, within touch. Since he belonged, even at the age of six, to that great clan which cannot
10 keep this feeling separate from that, but must let future prospects, with their joys and sorrows, cloud what is actually at hand, since to such people even in earliest childhood any turn in the wheel of sensation has the power to crystallize and transfix the moment upon which its gloom or radiance rests, James Ramsay, sitting on the floor cutting out pictures from the illustrated catalogue of the Army and Navy Stores, endowed the picture of a refrigerator as his mother spoke with heavenly bliss. It was fringed with joy. The wheelbarrow, the lawn-mover,
20 the sound of poplar trees, leaves whitening before rain, rooks cawing, brooms knocking, dresses rustling – all

these were so coloured and distinguished in his mind that he had already his private code, his secret language, though he appeared the image of stark and uncompromising severity, with his high forehead and his fierce blue eyes, impeccably candid and pure, frowning slightly at the sight of human frailty, so that his mother, watching him guide his scissors neatly round the refrigerator, imagined him all red and ermine on the Bench or directing a stern and momentous enterprise in some crisis of public affairs.

'But,' said his father, stopping in front of the drawing-room window, 'it won't be fine.'

Had there been an axe handy, a poker, or any weapon that would have gashed a hole in his father's breast and killed him, there and then, James would have seized it. Such were the extremes of emotion that Mr Ramsay excited in his children's breasts by his mere presence; standing, as now, lean as a knife, narrow as the blade of one, grinning sarcastically, not only with the pleasure of disillusioning his son and casting ridicule upon his wife, who was ten thousand times better in every way than he was (James thought), but also with some secret conceit at his own accuracy of judgement. What he said was true. It was always true. He was incapable of untruth; never tampered with a fact; never altered a disagreeable word to suit the pleasure or convenience of any mortal being, least of all of his own children, who, sprung from his loins, should be aware from childhood that life is difficult; facts uncompromising; and the passage to that fabled land where our brightest hopes are extinguished, our frail barks founder in darkness (here Mr Ramsay would straighten his back and narrow his little blue eyes upon the horizon), one that needs, above all, courage, truth, and the power to endure.

'But it may be fine – I expect it will be fine,' said Mrs Ramsay, making some little twist of the reddish-brown

60 stocking she was knitting, impatiently. If she finished it
tonight, if they did go to the Lighthouse after all, it was
to be given to the Lighthouse keeper for his little boy,
who was threatened with a tuberculous hip; together
with a pile of old magazines, and some tobacco, indeed
whatever she could find lying about, not really wanted,
but only littering the room, to give those poor fellows
who must be bored to death sitting all day with nothing
to do but polish the lamp and trim the wick and rake
about on their scrap of garden, something to amuse
them. For how would you like to be shut up for a whole
month at a time, and possibly more in stormy weather,
70 upon a rock the size of a tennis lawn? she would ask; and
to have no letters or newspapers, and to see nobody; if
you were married, not to see your wife, not to know how
your children were, – if they were ill, if they had fallen
down and broken their legs or arms; to see the same
dreary waves breaking week after week, and then a
dreadful storm coming, and the windows covered with
spray, and birds dashed against the lamp, and the whole
place rocking, and not be able to put your nose out of
doors for fear of being swept into the sea? How would
80 you like that? she asked, addressing herself particularly
to her daughters. So she added, rather differently, one
must take them whatever comforts one can.

'It's due west,' said the atheist Tansley, holding his
bony fingers spread so that wind blew through them, for
he was sharing Mr Ramsay's evening walk up and down,
up and down the terrace.

Virginia Woolf, *To the Lighthouse* (1927)

Here we are presented with a simple social interaction which
is interrupted by digressions. These take us into the minds of
different characters, revealing them and their thoughts about
each other, or into the mind of an unidentified narrator,

perhaps the author, who comments on the characters. We should first make clear what the central interaction consists of: it is but a brief conversation, begun by Mrs Ramsay, who remarks to her son that the expedition to the lighthouse might take place on the following day if the weather is fine though an early start will be necessary. Her husband says that it will not be fine. Mrs Ramsay demurs: 'But it may be fine – I expect it will be fine,' and is countered by Mr Tansley who asserts that the wind is due west. But how much more there is in the passage than that! The presence of such a range of material suggests that behind even the most casual moment of life there may lie a vast richness of reflection and response.

In the first long paragraph, notice the different perspectives on James's being. To begin with, we are given a keen sense of what passes through his mind: he is full of joy, so much so that even the picture that he is cutting out of a magazine, ironically the picture of a refrigerator, becomes 'endowed . . . with heavenly bliss'. Secondly, his personality is explained to us and categorised. We are told that he thinks by associating feelings with whatever happens to be around when the feeling occurs. He does not think by logic in a cold, cerebral way; he experiences life emotionally. A third perspective opens up when we see him through the eyes of his mother who 'imagined him all red and ermine on the Bench or directing a stern and momentous enterprise . . .' (lines 29–30). She sees him as a judge and she bases her fantasy of his future on his appearance, 'with his high forehead and his fierce blue eyes, impeccably candid and pure, frowning slightly at the sight of human frailty'. We, however, recognise that the inner reality of James's being does not match his mother's view of him. The last thing a judge should be is emotional.

There follows a moment's conversation before we are taken, via James's feelings about his father, into another assessment, this time of Mr Ramsay. The description of the man is not offered by James. Quite apart from its being far too sophisticated for a six-year-old, it is separated off from James by

'(James thought)' (line 43) which, in ascribing just one idea to the boy, places all other comments on Mr Ramsay in the mouth of some other speaker. We are told that he had 'some secret conceit at his own accuracy of judgement'. Who is the person offering this comment on Mr Ramsay? It is perhaps the same narrator who explained James to us. But notice what happens as this paragraph describing Mr Ramsay draws to a close (lines 48–55): the objective narrator ceases to speak in her own voice and gradually we sense that it is Mr Ramsay's characteristic manner of speaking that takes over. It is as if we are offered a glimpse of him – notice the description in brackets (lines 52–54) – and hear him utter some favourite sayings. Where do you think the transition from objective narrator to Mr Ramsay's style of speech occurs?

In all this analysis of methods, we might fail to respond to the sort of person Mr Ramsay is. He is a thinker who takes pleasure in telling the truth, however unpalatable it might be for his listeners. Moreover, he romanticises his hard philosophy of struggle and endurance narrowing 'his little blue eyes on the horizon', as if seeking distant truths, when describing the qualities that he so clearly believes he possesses: 'courage, truth, and the power to endure.' He is not made attractive to us and it is not surprising that James, who responds to life intuitively, through feeling, not by ignoring feelings, should find Mr Ramsay so repellent.

Finally, we turn to Mrs Ramsay, after a brief contribution to the conversation on which all this revelation of characters is hung. We learn of her present activity, the knitting of the stocking, and of her intentions for the following day and we learn what has prompted her thoughts. Mrs Ramsay is a sympathetic person, one who feels for the condition of others. She enters imaginatively into the experiences of the lighthouse keepers. Gradually we move from description of her present activity and thoughts into her *typical* utterances: 'she would ask' (line 70) establishes the more distant perspective. Her description of life in the lighthouse is detailed, impassioned, designed to produce a response and that response is to come, we find, from her daughters. It is they that she so preaches at, stirring them to take responsibility for the men. Why? Because she thinks that is an appropriate role for a woman? You will have to read more of the novel to find out the source of all that passionate concern in Mrs Ramsay. But notice here how, as if realising that she has been over-insistent, she is described as checking herself and concluding 'rather differently' (line 81) with her matter-of-fact final statement. This third digression completed, we turn back to the conversation and Tansley's observation on the unfavourable direction from which the wind blows.

I have called this section 'multiple consciousness' for, as the novel unfolds – and these are its opening pages – we come to see the characters from different points of view held, as far as is possible, simultaneously. It is a style of writing that might be compared with some twentieth-century paintings, for example, Picasso's cubist portraits, where the subject is painted face to face *and* in profile. This particularly modern way of looking at things implies that no one viewpoint leads us to the truth but rather that the truth about a character or situation is multi-faceted, only to be grasped by holding in tension a range of possible angles of vision.

Finally, here is a second passage from *To the Lighthouse* for you to appreciate. It occurs some twenty-five pages from the opening of the novel, the passage we have just been considering, and the circumstances of the characters are now a little clearer to us. They are all staying in the Ramsays' holiday home in Skye; Lily Briscoe and William Bankes are family friends and Andrew, Jasper and Rose are some of the Ramsays' children. There is also reference in this passage to the Swiss maid, Marie. **Write a detailed commentary on the extract, bringing out the following**:

1 the external events, the dialogue that actually happens during the time covered in this passage

2   the thoughts that pass through Mrs Ramsay's mind and
    their origin, whether they arise from people or circum-
    stances of the present or from her recent or more distant
    past
3   the understanding we gain of Mrs Ramsay's personality.

'And even if it isn't fine tomorrow,' said Mrs Ramsay,
raising her eyes to glance at William Bankes and Lily
Briscoe as they passed, 'it will be another day. And now,'
she said, thinking that Lily's charm was her Chinese
eyes, aslant in her white, puckered little face, but it
would take a clever man to see it, 'and now stand up,
and let me measure your leg,' for they might go to the
Lighthouse after all, and she must see if the stocking did
not need to be an inch or two longer in the leg.

10   Smiling, for an admirable idea had flashed upon her
this very second – William and Lily should marry – she
took the heather mixture stocking, with its criss-cross of
steel needles at the mouth of it, and measured it against
James's leg.

'My dear, stand still,' she said, for in his jealousy, not
liking to serve as measuring-block for the Lighthouse
keeper's little boy, James fidgeted purposely; and if he
did that, how could she see, was it too long, was it too
short? she asked.

20   She looked up – what demon possessed him, her
cherished? – and saw the room, saw the chairs, thought
them fearfully shabby. Their entrails, as Andrew said the
other day, were all over the floor; but then what was the
point, she asked herself, of buying good chairs to let them
spoil up here all through the winter when the house, with
only one old woman to see to it, positively dripped with
wet? Never mind: the rent was precisely twopence half-
penny; the children loved it; it did her husband good to
be three thousand, or if she must be accurate, three

30   hundred miles from his library and his lectures and his disciples; and there was room for visitors. Mats, camp beds, crazy ghosts of chairs and tables whose London life of service was done – they did well enough here; and a photograph or two, and books. Books, she thought, grew of themselves. She never had time to read them. Alas! even the books that had been given her, and inscribed by the hand of the poet himself: 'For her whose wishes must be obeyed' ... 'The happier Helen of our day' ... disgraceful to say, she had never read them. And
40   Croom on the Mind and Bates on the Savage Customs of Polynesia ('My dear, stand still,' she said) – neither of those could one send to the Lighthouse. At a certain moment, she supposed, the house would become so shabby that something must be done. If they could be taught to wipe their feet and not bring the beach in with them – that would be something. Crabs, she had to allow, if Andrew really wished to dissect them, or if Jasper believed that one could make soup from seaweed, one could not prevent it; or Rose's objects – shells, reeds,
50   stones; for they were gifted, her children, but all in quite different ways. And the result of it was, she sighed, taking in the whole room from floor to ceiling, as she held the stocking against James's leg, that things got shabbier and got shabbier summer after summer. The mat was fading; the wallpaper was flapping. You couldn't tell any more that those were roses on it. Still, if every door in a house is left perpetually open, and no lockmaker in the whole of Scotland can mend a bolt, things must spoil. What was the use of flinging a green Cashmere shawl
60   over the edge of a picture frame? In two weeks it would be the colour of pea soup. But it was the doors that annoyed her; every door was left open. She listened. The drawing-room door was open; the hall door was open; it sounded as if the bedroom doors were open; and certainly the window on the landing was open, for that

she had opened herself. That windows should be open, and doors shut — simple as it was, could none of them remember it? She would go into the maids' bedrooms at night and find them sealed like ovens, except for Marie's the Swiss girl, who would rather go without a bath than without fresh air, but then at home, she had said, 'the mountains are so beautiful'. She had said that last night looking out of the window with tears in her eyes. 'The mountains are so beautiful.' Her father was dying there, Mrs Ramsay knew. He was leaving them fatherless. Scolding and demonstrating (how to make a bed, how to open a window, with hands that shut and spread like a Frenchwoman's) all had folded itself quietly about her, when the girl spoke, as, after a flight through the sunshine the wings of a bird fold themselves quietly and the blue of its plumage changes from bright steel to soft purple. She had stood there silent for there was nothing to be said. He had cancer of the throat. At the recollection — how she had stood there, how the girl had said 'At home the mountains are so beautiful', and there was no hope, no hope whatever, she had a spasm of irritation, and speaking sharply, said to James:

'Stand still. Don't be tiresome,' so that he knew instantly that her severity was real, and straightened his leg and she measured it.

The stocking was too short by half an inch at least, making allowance for the fact that Sorley's little boy would be less well grown than James.

'It's too short,' she said, 'ever so much too short.'

Never did anybody look so sad. Bitter and black, halfway down, in the darkness, in the shaft which ran from the sunlight to the depths, perhaps a tear formed; a tear fell; the waters swayed this way and that, received it, and were at rest. Never did anybody look so sad.

Virginia Woolf, *To the Lighthouse* (1927)

Index